Crazy Wolf

A Half-Breed Story

by
John Spence, PhD

Praise for *Crazy Wolf: A Half Breed Story*

What a pleasure to read this honest and heartfelt account of a life well lived despite adverse conditions. John is a humble man whose accomplishments, influence, and exploits actually exceed his telling. It's a rare quality for an Indian storyteller to tell an engaging and compelling story without embellishing. This work honors his friends, family, and colleagues with recognition and gratitude. He tells the truth and makes us smile. The reach of his influence goes far and wide in Indian Country. I know, because, as one of his students, I would never have been able to walk my path without his encouragement.
— Terry L. Cross, (Seneca Nation), DHL (hon), MSW, ACSW, LCSW
Founder & Senior Advisor,
National Indian Child Welfare Association

An intriguing life story about pain, joy and discovery leading to numerous accomplishments. As a half breed myself I felt absorbed by John's story relating to his journey. Over the years my tribe has requested his assistance with several grant writing projects and help with horse therapy workshops at our summer youth culture camps.
— Caroline Cruz (Warm Springs)
General Manager, Health and Human Services
Confederated Tribes of the Warm Springs Reservation of Oregon

John takes you on a journey of deep compassion, sadness, hope and joy as he paints a vivid picture of the lasting impacts of historical and intergenerational trauma, healing and wisdom. Through his personal mantra of "Opportunity, Effort and Ability," we recognize his strong instinct and feel his desire to be a better human being, to be of service to others and to seek and manifest social justice. Every Native parent, schoolteacher, social worker, public health professional, tribal council member, urban Natives and anyone wishing to be trauma and healing informed should read John's story. John has been a mentor and hero of mine for decades and now even more after reading his powerful and heartfelt memoir. Crazy Wolf is a natural leader and his teachings will continue on through *Crazy Wolf: A Half-Breed Story*.
— Jillene Joseph (A'aniiih)
Founder and Executive Director, The Native Wellness Institute

This is an incredible autobiography of a man born into extreme poverty and alcoholism on an isolated Indian reservation and then to urban low-income housing projects where he experiences racism and economic disparities at an early age. His story highlights the major changes in the social and political history in Indian country in which he lives, and establishes a sense of self-identity based on his life experiences. His life journey is a study of internal resistance and perseverance during adverse situations. His life experiences leads to a productive life helping others through the tools that assisted him into becoming a scholar, advocate for social causes, and staunch supporter of those in recovery.

— Phillip Shortman, PhD (Gros Ventre)
Former Fort Belknap Tribal Councilman and Vietnam Veteran
Holder of the Distinguished Service Cross and Silver Star

Crazy Wolf: A Half-Breed Story opens the heart in a delightful yet serious life journey of a man born in difficult circumstances who managed to overcome poverty, stigma, historical trauma, and racism. The path from chaotic reservation, to city low-income housing, to drifting for direction, and finally finding success and comfort is a story for Native and non-Natives alike, especially for those struggling with similar life events. It's a good read... "Let's go people."

— Dale Walker, MD (Cherokee Nation)
Former President, Association of American Indian Physicians

John has done a great job of portraying life in and out of reservation scenarios and in and out of alcoholic situations. In his autobiography he is thoughtful for folks who came into his life, especially BJ and his healer Koda, and his many friends made while he lived life. Through his athletic ability and kinship with others, he developed into a kind and thoughtful man yet this value was always there, just beneath the skin. It's truly difficult to understand how a half breed Indian who has been disenfranchised early on in life can eventually be whole and feel free to be who he is.

— Patrick Weasel Head (Blackfeet), PhD
Former Missoula City Councilman and Vietnam Veteran

ISBN: 978-1-7363843-1-2 (print)
ISBN: 978-1-7363843-2-9 (epub)
ISBN: 978-1-7363843-3-6 (mobi)

KMC Media Co.
Portland, Oregon

Book design by Julie Murkette

Cover photo from collection of Marsha Spence Furfaro (n.d.)

*Freedom comes as winter settles in his heart
and he is at peace with the seasons.*

— John Wesley Contway
Red Shadows of the Blood Moon

For Marsha, a beautiful earth woman who keeps the family together
For Avis, a pipe carrier who sacrifices and pours water for the people
For BJ, a dancer
For Erik, who has forgiven his father
For Joy, who never backs down
For angels on earth, who are my grandchildren
For Koda, who teaches us horse medicine
For Ruby, who taught pure doggie love
For nieces and nephews, who laugh and run everywhere
For Native mothers and aunts, who always carry our burden
For Native fathers and uncles, who have survived
and for Mollie Cochran Archambault who saved us all.

Molly Cochran Archambault (n.d.)
Marsha Spence Furfaro photo collection

Introduction

Indians love stories. It's how we learn about our family and tribal histories and our unwritten taboos and protocols. We spend a lot of time visiting about who we're related to, who someone else is related to, and whose paternity is questionable. A friend, Cecilia Fire Thunder (Lakota) once called this our "sacred gossip." It's our stories of who we are.

I was given the Indian name Crazy Wolf by an uncle, but not in a formal traditional ceremony. He was just joking around, but the name stuck. That's because wolves maintain an extremely close family structure so there's something wrong, or crazy, about a wolf who keeps to himself.

This name fits me. I'm an introvert who is way more comfortable being by myself or around animals than being around a lot of people. I was a real backward and fearful kid who always ran away down to the creek to hide in the brush when people came by to visit. What follows is my story—a parentless, half-breed Indian whose Indian half has always been the dominant part of the story.

Table of Contents

Chapter 1
How Do We Forgive Our Fathers

A guy I know once said in an AA meeting that he became an alcoholic when he was two years old. That's when his father left the family. I sat there thinking, that's kind of like me. My mother died in 1944 when I was three years old and I never met my biological father. I have two older sisters and my mother never officially married any of our three birth fathers. So, technically, I'm just another illegitimate half-breed kid from an Indian reservation in Montana.

My birth father never acknowledged me and I never met him. My stepfather, John Spence ("Dear John" as he was called by his friends) was never around to take care of my two older sisters and me. Dear John was an old rodeo cowboy, and a shiftless ranch hand who ended up training and shoeing horses on the smaller horse racing tracks around Montana and the northwest states. He was a Piegan Indian from Canada who ran away from an orphanage at age 13. I heard he was adopted by a white ranching family somewhere across the Medicine Line (the Canadian border) a little north of my relatives' home in Montana.

Due to abandonment by both my birth father and stepfather, and loss of my mother at an early age, I developed the attachment disorder, fears, and survival skills typical of so many other half-breed kids on my reservation and throughout Indian Country.

1

Excessive drinking is often a symptom of our Indigenous sadness and loss, and the generational soul wound that is inescapable in our DNA. I was no exception from this destructive way of coping. Alcohol would eventually become my medicine to help alleviate the shame, fears, and social anxiety that I lived with.

I never knew my stepfather's real story. He rarely visited my two older sisters and me when we stayed with relatives on the Fort Belknap Indian Reservation or when we lived in the little border town of Harlem, Montana. Without parents around, our grandparents and an uncle looked after my sisters and me both emotionally and financially. Even today in most tribal and urban Indian communities, it's pretty common for grandparents or aunts and uncles to raise the kids.

My stepdad never paid child support of any kind to our grandparents. The only gift I ever received from him was a leather wallet when I was about six or seven years old and we were living in Harlem. Naturally there wasn't any money in it.

We didn't look alike and I always knew my stepfather didn't care about me. I figured he wasn't my real father, even though my suspicions were always dismissed. Like so many others, our reservation Indian family has a hard-wired denial system. Rumors I'd overheard as a child that John Spence Sr. wasn't my biological father were sternly rejected by my grandmother and a favorite aunt whenever I tried to bring it up. This prevented me from confirming my questionable paternity until I went home to work at Fort Belknap as the tribal health planner in 1980 and learned more about my personal history.

That was when one of my cousins on the tribal council, Jessie James Hawley, encouraged me to meet other relatives on my birth father's side to learn more about my personal history. I was really nervous about approaching these folks, but my fears were allayed when I visited some relatives suggested by Jessie who I hadn't met before. I was surprised at how warmly they welcomed me. A few even agreed to sign official paternity affidavits about my true lineage. This was also verified by the Fort Belknap Agency Superintendent, Elmer Main, from his personal knowledge that Dear John wasn't my biological dad. Due to this research and help from others, my Certificate of Degree of Indian Blood (CDIB) was eventually changed to one-half degree Indian blood on my reservation enrollment card during 1982.

Both of my long deceased birth parents are recorded as one-half Indian on our reservation agency rolls kept by the Bureau of Indian Affairs (BIA). With the new CDIB, I became officially a half-breed Indian . . . half Indian and half white. My tribal enrollment card lists me as 3/8 Gros Ventre (A'aninin) and 1/8 Sioux (Hunkpapa Lakota). With the change in blood quantum to 1/2, this increased my son Erik's status to 1/4 and I was then able to have him enrolled in 1994.

I never learned why my birth father wasn't interested in meeting me. It's one of those dysfunctional reservation family secrets we learn to live with—"don't talk, don't trust, don't feel." Still, I never really developed a big resentment against him for not being around as a father figure. My uncles fit that role . . . except for their drinking and frequent absences from our families. Without a lot of healthy adult Indian male role models, this probably resulted in my later problems with intimacy in adult relationships. Anyway, not having a father never felt like it was worth crying about.

I was too young to remember much about our mother, Sybil Cochran Archambault, but I still remember when a train brought her home to Harlem. She had gone to Seattle to work in a defense plant during WWII while my two older sisters and I stayed home in Harlem with our grandparents, Sam Archambault and Molly Cochran Archambault. I was three years old then in 1944 and we were all living in Harlem when we received a telegram. Our mother had been struck and killed by a U.S. mail truck while crossing a street in downtown Seattle.

I don't remember all the devastation our family felt at the time, but that train is still embedded in my memory. Even today a train whistle is one of the saddest sounds for me.

The train that brought our mother home doesn't stop in Harlem anymore. The town's population has shrunk from a high of 1,267 in 1960 to 823 in 2016. Harlem is now just another small prairie town where *The Grand* theater has played the last picture show, Merle's Confectionary next door is boarded up, and the Ford dealer left town.

When I was entering the 3rd grade we moved from Harlem because my uncle, Bryan Cochran Archambault, a WWII veteran, got a job in Seattle. My two older sisters and grandmother and I moved there with him through a government program called Relocation that began after the war.

We ended up in a low-income housing project in South Seattle called Lakewood. It was full of brown and Indigenous people and a lot of Indian families like us who were on welfare. That project would probably now be called a ghetto, but we were welcomed there and it really expanded the world for my sisters and me. Our relatives from Montana, however, often came to visit us and brought their drinking with them to continue our poverty and shame.

There was a community center in the Lakewood project where a Black guy named Lee was the director. Lee was kind to all of us project kids and he tried his best to bring movies, dances, arts and crafts, and other creative activities for us. There was also a small lake next to the project where I learned to swim. In the summers all of us project kids spent lots of time at that lake. Once Lee and another staff member took several of us boys with them for a fishing weekend at a cabin on a lake somewhere outside the city. That was a great time, one of the highlights from my five years of living in the Lakewood project.

During summers we also enjoyed exploring and sleeping out in the woods next to the project. None of us kids could afford private summer camps where fees were charged, and we couldn't afford tents. So we just slept out in the trees and made small campfires where baked potatoes in tinfoil was our main treat. We didn't know about smores or camp songs that other kids in school were familiar with, but we still had a good time.

All the project kids were either on welfare or lived below the federal poverty level. For spending money or school clothes we caught buses for long rides out to work in the fields to pick beans and strawberries in the summer. We also used to fish in the Duwamish River for shiners. This a small fish that we sold for 25 cents each to an elderly Japanese gentleman who lived in the project.

The five years in the Lakewood project provided a temporary community of mostly happy memories and adventures for my two older sisters and me. It was only our Indian relatives' drinking and the shame and fear it caused us that spoiled the memories of those years in the project.

Just before I entered the 8th grade my uncle Bryan Cochran Archambault was able to buy a house a little further south of Seattle in a small community called Des Moines. My two sisters and I then attended schools in the town of Burien.

I was 16 years old the summer after my sophomore year in high school and was really surprised one day. My stepfather John Spence (Dear John) called out of the blue and asked if I had a summer job yet. When I said that I didn't, he asked me to come down to help him work at the horse racing track in Portland, Oregon. Despite my resentment toward him, I thought what the heck, this might be interesting. I then caught the Greyhound bus to Portland where he and his live-in girlfriend met me.

Alma, the girlfriend, was a horse trainer and a kind woman who was immediately likable. Alma was tough. I remember a time when she defeated a mouthy male jockey in a spontaneous wrestling match. They tangled in the dirt and sawdust next to some horse stalls while a small crowd gathered around cheering her on and howling with laughter. Alma became a buffer between me and the old man and she helped us navigate the uncomfortable silence between us. I always appreciated her and regretted their parting a few years later.

During those two summers with Dear John and Alma we hauled horses from the racetrack at Portland to Tillamook, Oregon, then to Seattle, and finally to a couple of small racetracks around Vancouver, B.C. It soon became clear that my stepfather wasn't interested in knowing me better. He really just wanted me around for cheap labor with the race horses. I earned $100 per month while paying for most of my own food and sleeping on an old army cot in a smelly tack room between horse stalls.

The horses would keep me up nights kicking the stalls, stomping, and snorting. Our grain and oat barrels attracted mice and they also kept me up. If the mice got too noisy at night I would throw old paperbacks at them from a cardboard box full of western novels that a friendly old groom named Bud had given me. Without a radio or television in the tack room and just a bare light bulb I read a lot of those books at night.

With his drinking and selfishness, these two summers working on the racetracks failed to promote any happy paternal bond from developing between my stepfather and me. So one day nearing the end of the second summer I decided I'd had enough of him and the racetrack life. One of our horse owners, Bun Purcell, had earlier offered me a job at a plywood mill that he owned in Tillamook and I accepted it.

Those next two summers working in the plywood mill at Tillamook were a pretty lonely existence, but I earned more than working on the racetrack. The Oregon coast was beautiful and I didn't have to put up with Dear John and sleep in a dusty tack room with mice for roommates. I was only 18 that first summer in Tillamook and I didn't have any access to alcohol, except one weekend when two high school friends came down from Seattle to visit. They brought lots of Olympia beer with them and we got wasted near a small beach town called Netarts.

My childhood story isn't very unique in Indian Country, even today. Many Indian kids still grow up with absent, alcoholic, or disinterested fathers. Many of our fathers are those sad, annoying drunks on 1st Avenue in Seattle, on Burnside in Portland, and in other cities and reservation border towns. These are the fallen warriors the American empire has left behind.

How Do We Forgive Our Fathers

How do we forgive our Fathers?
Maybe in a dream
Do we forgive our Fathers for leaving us too often or forever
when we were little?

Maybe for scaring us with unexpected rage
or making us nervous
because there never seemed to be any rage there at all.

Do we forgive our Fathers for marrying
or not marrying our Mothers?
For divorcing or not divorcing our Mothers?

And shall we forgive them for their excesses of warmth or
coldness?
Shall we forgive them for pushing or leaning
for shutting doors
for speaking through walls
or never speaking or never being silent?

Do we forgive our Fathers in our age or in theirs
or their deaths
saying it to them or not saying it?

If we forgive our fathers what is left?

— Reprinted with permission from
Dick Lourie and Hanging Loose Press (1998)

Our mother, Sybil Cochran Archambault (n.d.)
Marsha Spence Furfaro photo collection

Dear John (n.d.)
Marsha Spence Furfaro photo collection

Chapter 2
Nobody Loves a Drunken Indian

There is a good description of my family and relatives' lives in the border town of Harlem and on the Fort Belknap Indian Reservation during the 1940s through the 60s. It is written with stark realism by John Wesley Contway (Lakota) in his book *Red Shadows of the Blood Moon* (2016, Trafford Publishing).

Contway, aka "Big John," describes the racism and classism experienced by half-breed Indians like him and me, and his account is painfully accurate. He describes our families' reaction to this as follows: "Alcohol has become the honorary tribal member that makes us cheat and lie for the numbness of our pain."

During our childhoods in Harlem and on the Fort Belknap Indian Reservation, our families were caught in a spirit crushing bind of poverty, alcoholism, prejudice, and denial for half-breeds like Big John and me. While continuing his tale of life in Harlem and Fort Belknap during the times of our childhoods, he says, "Every Indian story is a sad story. There was nothing expected other than living in chaos, poverty and alcoholic despair."

Throughout his book Big John repeats that line, "Every Indian story is a sad story." When I shared with him over Facebook that I was writing a memoir, he told me not to forget to include that line . . . "Every Indian story is a sad story." After reading a couple of chapters of my first draft, he gave me a boost by saying it was better than "that Sherman [Alexie] guy," but he also said I needed to include more "Indin humor."

This period of time and locale were also described earlier by James Welch (Blackfeet/Gros Ventre) in his poem *Harlem, Montana: Just Off the Reservation*: "Booze is law and all the Indians drink in the best tavern . . . Harlem, so bigoted you forgot the latest joke." (from *Riding the Earthboy 40*, 1971).

The racism directed at Indian families in Harlem and around Montana while our grandmother was growing up had many lingering effects for us kids. Even with all the childhood trauma and racism she had experienced, my grandmother was still one of the strongest and wisest Indian women I've known. She embodied the best of our Native cultural values of generosity and non-judgmental behavior. As a child our grandmother ran away so many times from the Catholic boarding school at the St. Paul Mission in Hays, Montana that the agency authorities finally gave up trying to bring her back. Even with that experience, however, she still made my two older sisters and I attend the St. Thomas Catholic Church in Harlem, and we hated it.

We were poor, dark, and our clothes were too shabby for some of the good white ladies in that church. One time my sister Marsha overheard two of them tell the priest they would quit attending church if "those dirty little Indians" didn't sit in the back. The only good thing I remember about that church was the free lunch they gave us in the summer, although the baloney sandwiches were pretty dry. After our first communion in Harlem we had enough of the Catholic Church and our grandmother didn't force us to go anymore. I've attended other churches since then, but Christianity doesn't work for me.

During our childhood in Harlem my sisters and I would often wait in the car outside a famous Indian bar in Harlem called Beanie's. Our grandparents, uncles, aunts, and other relatives drank there to have a little fun and drown away their pain. It was boring and a little scary for us to sit outside the bar, but it was still fun sometimes to hear their gossip and laughter. That is, until the inevitable crying jags and fights and misery started.

Sometimes while we waited outside Beanie's the folks would bring out chips and pop for us kids, or give us a few coins to walk over to a small store on the east side of town for treats. Occasionally the folks would also give us coins for the slot machines in Beanie's. It wasn't legal for us kids to play slot machines, or even to be in the bar, but no one seemed to care.

When our relatives or other Indians passed out in the tall grass behind Beanie's, us kids would step over the fallen bodies of these defeated warriors and pick up empty beer bottles to sell in town for candy or snacks. Beanie's was one of the most well-known Indian bars in Montana, but it burned down several years ago. Now only an empty lot sits there in the middle of town next to the boarded-up businesses on main street Harlem.

Today Harlem is not as bad for Indians as it used to be and many Indian families live there. Indian students comprise about 70% of the high school and some Indian parents have even been on the school board. During football and basketball games Indian folks from the reservation and the white people in town and from nearby farms and ranches cheer equally for the home team. During these games our usual animosity towards each other is put aside, and just for a little while, we actually look like one harmonious community.

Our good times as kids were mostly on the reservation at Fort Belknap. When our relatives weren't scaring us with their drinking and we had enough to eat, it was almost a paradise. We could run around "like wild Indians" everywhere around the community of Old Hays without any adult supervision. The creek, hills, and mountains held endless adventures.

Trout fishing was good in the creek at Old Hays on the south end of the reservation and up behind the beaver dams in Mission Canyon in the Little Rocky Mountains. My uncle Bryan Cochran Archambault was a "fish whisperer"—real knowledgeable and stealthy and always able to catch more fish than the rest of us. The water table for that creek, however, has been lowered considerably and the upper reaches contain too many toxins. This is due to our ground water being used for an open pit gold mining operation on a mountain at the head waters. The Pegasus Mining Company eventually pulled out of there after stealing our water and leaving cyanide mine tailings to leech into the creek.

Despite their drinking, I used to love to tag along when my uncles were hunting deer in the mountains or sage hens out on the prairie. They also used to take me fishing on the Missouri River across the Little Rockies just south of the old mining towns of Landusky and Zortman. The river was our reservation's south boundary at one time, but gold was discovered in the Little Rockies near there and the federal government took that land away.

Compensation for losing the land in the Little Rockies or the damage done by the Pegasus Mining Company never happened. Our tribe learned that the "Doctrine of Discovery" and "Manifest Destiny" are still the law of the land in the USA when it comes to Indians. Our treaty of 1888 with the federal government that created the original south boundary of our reservation just north of the Missouri River meant nothing.

At Old Hays us kids looked forward to track meets and fireworks that one of our uncles, Sonny Cochran, used to organize in the summer. Then in the winter we loved sledding down the surrounding hills in old car fenders when we didn't have proper sleds. The house parties in Hays when our relatives would break out fiddles and guitars were also fun—except when the folks' drinking became really scary for us kids.

Sherman Alexie in his powerful memoir titled *You Don't Have to Say You Love Me* (2017, Little Brown) describes how as a kid on his reservation his parents hosted a "potentially lethal" New Year's Eve party that made him and his sisters afraid of being assaulted by drunken adult friends and relatives. "My monsters had brown skin, dark hair and eyes, and they looked like me." That was exactly how my sisters and I were often afraid of our own drunken adult relatives. It wasn't just from the monsters in our grandmother's ghost stories.

Our relatives' music parties were also held in some cabins up in the Mission Canyon in the Little Rockies. The mountains there were a perfect playground for all of us kids. Unfortunately, either the Bureau of Indian Affairs or the tribal council sold those cabins. While living in Seattle later we still missed the reservation a lot and always wanted to go home. Most Indians are pretty transitory and that was true for us. I remember many all-night driving trips back to Montana when my sisters and I were filled with anticipation. We travelled back to the reservation whenever my uncle could get off work at Boeing.

There were often wall-to-wall Indians sleeping off a drunk on our floor when we were living back in Harlem or at Hays on the reservation during the 1940s. This continued at the housing project in Seattle when we moved there in 1949. In the city during the 1950s it was often the same thing as back home on the reservation. My sisters and I were often ashamed to bring home our school friends when drunk relatives were visiting.

The stresses and fears I felt due to our general insecurity and the folks' drinking probably led to my night terrors and bed wetting during my early elementary school years, especially when we lived in Harlem and Havre. My uncle and sisters often had to restrain me while yelling, slashing around, and sleep walking. Fortunately, I managed to outgrow the nightmares and bed wetting around early adolescence while we were still living in the Lakewood Project.

During elementary school years in Harlem and in the project in Seattle, my sisters and I experienced significant racism and class discrimination as just another Indian family on welfare. We had dark skin, we were poor, and we didn't have a mother or father like most of the other kids. The feeling of being an "other," someone less than, contributed to me feeling more inferior to white Americans. It was hard for me to shake this negative self image throughout my adolescence and early adult years.

A book titled *Nobody Loves a Drunken Indian* was published in 1967 and later a movie called *Flap* based on the book was released in 1970. While there was some humor in both the book and the movie, this furthered the stereotype of drunken Indians and reservation despair.

My early shame, anger and fears led to a drive to accomplish some things that were not to be expected from an introverted, parentless, poor, half-breed Indian kid like me. Things that happened for me later like going to college, ocean lifeguarding, the Marine Corps, grad school, rugby, Indian rodeo, a doctoral program, and triathlon were all challenges that didn't just sort of fall into place.

Looking back on my childhood on the reservation and in the project, I'm reminded of words to a song from 1973 called "Reservation of Education" by the Indigenous band XIT:

> You've been born into a world of sorrow
> You've been born to try and change tomorrow . . . .
> Oh I was told my way was wrong
> And I must change to get along.

So, a personal prayer developed for me. I prayed first for the opportunity, then the effort to try whatever the challenge was, and finally for the ability to do it. A three-part internal prayer/mantra evolved for me over the years and I still summon it often—opportunity, effort, ability.

I also owe a lot to many people. I couldn't have accomplished much without the help, support, and kindness of others. In this narrative I want to point out and thank the many beautiful and gracious people who have helped me on this journey.

Snake Butte and Buffalo just south of Harlem, Montana (2020)
Randy Perez photo collection

Mission Canyon at Hays, Montana (2020)
Stephanie Thornley photo collection

Chapter 3
My Old School

Things began to improve for me and my two sisters when my uncle, Brian Cochran Archambault, was able to buy a small house in the Seattle suburb of Des Moines and we all moved with him and our grandmother from the Lakewood project. My sister Marsha and I then went to junior high and high school in the community of Burien. Our older sister Avis attended high school there for a short time, but she dropped out of school to work on a race track in California with Dear John (her birth father). Soon after that she married a jockey and she has lived in Arizona with her family ever since then.

The racism and rejection that my sisters and I experienced in Harlem and in the housing project in Seattle was much less while attending two schools in Burien. For a parentless half-breed Indian kid like me, with low self-esteem and on welfare, this was a unique experience. Junior high and high school, therefore, became a turning point for me. For the first time I began to feel a little better about myself.

Despite our better experiences in junior high and high school, our classmates in Burien never knew how out of place Marsha and I felt in school. These schools in Burien were more welcoming for us, but they were way less racially diverse than the two elementary schools we had attended next to the Lakewood project.

There was only one other Indian kid in our new school in Burien, Robin Young. He and I were on the swim team together at Sylvester Junior High and we later graduated together from Highline High School. Robin and I were always friendly and supportive of each other, but not especially close. He later became an accomplished totem pole carver and one of his works is prominently displayed in West Seattle today.

In high school there was only one Black student, Bobby Shaw, who was a year ahead of me in school. He and I had been close friends during our time living next to each other in the Lakewood project during the third through seventh grades, but we lived too far away from each other during high school to hang out a lot together.

At Sylvester Junior High there was one white kid who was bigger than me and tried to bully me. I'd had enough of this and finally told him to meet me after school. He never showed up, and that was the end of that. Otherwise, junior high was mostly a good experience for me, but moving up to Highline High School was even better. There was only one time in high school that an older football player always seemed to have a sour attitude around me, but it never got around to a fist fight. I only got into one unremarkable fist fight in high school with another guy in my class. It was over a girl we were both interested in. Neither one of us won the fight or the girl. Years later this guy and I hugged and had a good laugh about it.

There were several white students in junior and senior high school who were very accepting of me and we became friends. These former classmates always bring back good memories: Steven Barlow, Dick Blackwood, Dave Burpee, Margie Conrad, Judy Dugan, Mike Gallando, Terry Hildebrand, Steve Holtschalg,

Gary Jarvis, Jackie Kuehn, Tom Lindeman, John Magnuson, Mike Makar, Bill Martin, Jim and Judy McBride, Jon MacLure, Katie Meany, Ron Sather, Gordy Shaw, Martin Simonsen, Nancy Smallwood, Loren Tomlinson.

There were many others with whom I wasn't real close, but most were respectful when greeting me and others. These fellow students helped me realize that the world wasn't always a totally cold and hostile place for Indian kids like me who didn't fit the white All-American stereotype.

One of my junior varsity football coaches at Highline High, Mr. Lowell Quesnell, even invited me to go with him to the school's Father-Son Banquet during junior year. I never knew how he'd heard I didn't have a father, but I really appreciated his kindness—especially coming from a tough old football coach like him. Mr. Quenelle and Mr. Shawls, our two JV coaches, were "players' coaches"—good guys who treated us with respect, not like the grumpy head varsity coach. I had fun playing JV football and caught lots of passes. Once after catching a real long pass Mr. Shawls started calling me "R.C. Spence" (after a San Francisco 49er football player named R.C. Owen).

Our senior year Homecoming football program listed me as a senior end at 5'9" and 160 lbs., but I was actually 5'10" and only a little over 140 lbs.—probably too small and skinny really for a school with almost 2,000 students. I wasn't playing much during senior year and didn't like the varsity head coach, so I quit football right before our Homecoming game. The two other senior ends who were playing more than me, Steve Holtschlag and Jim Magneson, were both good friends and a lot bigger than me. Afterward, I regretted quitting and not finishing with football in high school. This experience made me more grateful to begin playing rugby later when I was still 5'10", but about 175-80 lbs. after taking weight training in college and surviving Marine Corps boot camp.

The other high school sports regret was letting down our track coach, Mr. Carpine. During sophomore year he was my Physical Education teacher and said that since I was a pretty fast runner he'd give me an A for the class if I came out for the track team in the spring. I told him I would and received the A, but instead of following through with my commitment to Mr. Carpine I chose to drink and party around that spring. These two sports regrets in football and track later influenced me to not quit with commitments I'd made to myself and others.

During senior year a teacher, Mr. Glen Hagen, and a school counselor, Mr. Earl Trowbridge, started talking to me about college. This felt pretty strange. None of my relatives had gone to college so it wasn't something I'd even dreamed about as a possibility before this. I thought college was just for rich white kids.

As an Indian kid on welfare my main concerns were just acceptance from my peers, finishing school, and getting some kind of job after graduation so I wouldn't be poor anymore. College wasn't even a thought until Mr. Hagen and Mr. Trowbridge encouraged me to complete an admission application to the University of Washington and apply for two small scholarship sources they had found. With their help I was accepted at the UW and the two scholarships applications were successful—all thanks to those two kind gentlemen at Highline High.

There were other changes during my last year in high school which were quite impactful. First, my uncle, Bryan Cochran Archambault, had gotten married and my two older sisters moved out of his house in Des Moines during the summer just before my senior year while I was working on the race tracks. My grandmother and I also moved out at that time. We found a small house near the Seattle airport during my last year at Highline High School.

Most of my white classmates didn't know it was only my grandmother and me living together during my senior year, and that we were receiving a public welfare grant called ADC (Aid to Dependent Children). Being parentless was bad enough and I was too ashamed to reveal my poverty status to my classmates. I never told anyone about the one month that winter of senior year when we ran short on money. We could either buy food or pay for heat. We chose food for that month and just bundled up under more blankets.

Then came high school graduation. It was mostly a happy time and I began to look forward to the new adventures that college would bring. Another tragic loss struck my family, however, that nearly derailed everything. My uncle committed suicide about a week before graduation. This was my mother's brother, the fish whisperer, a WWII veteran, the man who had sacrificed so much to support my grandmother and raise my sisters and me. His drinking had finally gotten him fired at Boeing and he must have thought there was no way out.

Years later at a high school reunion a close friend and football teammate, Steve Holtschlag, remarked how he was the only blond-headed white kid at my uncle's funeral just before our graduation. I'd forgotten that Steve had gone to the funeral to support me, and his presence there was completely blocked from my memory for years. Losing my uncle Bryan must have been more traumatic than I realized at the time. I've since discovered that grief and loss make us feel like we're not a part of everyday reality for a while and we lose parts of time and memories.

High school graduation and turning 18 years old also meant the Aid to Dependent Children welfare grant for my grandmother and me would come to an end. In those days there was no safety net or transitional program of any kind once a welfare kid turned 18. It was sink or swim in a hostile white world for Indian kids like me.

Fortunately, this would be the start of two summer jobs working in the plywood mill at Tillamook. A few days after graduation I drove down to the Oregon coast in my old 1939 Chevy with another one of our uncles from Montana who was visiting our family at the time. After we made it to Tillamook my uncle, Ed Archambault, caught a bus back to Seattle.

At age 18, out of high school and broke, I was truly on my own for the first time. After the death of my uncle Bryan, and living without my grandmother and sisters, the summer of 1959 was one of the saddest and loneliest periods of my life thus far.

Highline High School, Junior Year (1957-58)
Marsha Spence Furfaro photo collection

Chapter 4
An Indian in College

During 1959-60, my first year at the University of Washington, I only saw four other Indians on the campus of 30,000 students. This was because we each received financial help from the United Scholarship Service in Denver. There might have been more than us five Indian students, but I didn't recognize any others, and in those days there was no Native American Studies Program or other Indian student support program on campus.

An impressive Indian woman from the United Scholarship Service, Tillie Walker, would visit the five of us occasionally to see how we were doing. Once she showed up on crutches and in a leg cast due to a snow skiing accident. Tillie was the first Indian I'd ever heard of who skied. I thought that skiing was only for rich white kids. A few years later I learned to ski and met Charlie Scott, an Alaskan Native. Charlie competed in downhill ski racing and also rode bulls and bucking horses in Indian rodeos.

There was another small scholarship that I received from the Highline Savings and Loan Bank in Burien. These two scholarships gave me a foundation to start college that I supplemented by working each summer and part-time work on campus every academic quarter.

The two scholarships weren't enough to pay for tuition and books while living on campus so I worked two summers at the plywood mill at Tillamook and then two summers lifeguarding at Seaside, Oregon. I also worked part-time every academic quarter by washing dishes, waiting tables, delivering furniture, or delivering flowers. This allowed me to graduate in a little over four years without any student loans or debts to pay. My tribe at Fort Belknap didn't assist with any of my college education. That's probably because I didn't have parents at the reservation to advocate for a Bureau of Indian Affairs (BIA) higher education scholarship for me.

In-state tuition and the cost of books at the UW during 1959-63 weren't as outrageous as they are now. Another reason I was also able to survive in college was due to the help of two great guys at the UW who had graduated from Highline High School three years before me. These two, Sonny Matson and Chuck Cooper, encouraged me to join them in Theta Chi Fraternity. By doing this, I only had to pay half the monthly room and board cost I would normally have paid to stay in a dorm. This was because another guy and I took turns washing dishes for three years at the fraternity house in exchange for one-half the boarding costs per month.

Cooper started calling me "The Fast Indian" when I was playing intramural football with him and some other guys in the fraternity. This was one nick name I didn't mind having—after all, I could run pretty fast on the football field. The guys in the house accepted me without prejudice, even though I was the only Indian and they knew I didn't have parents and came from a poverty background. Some of the guys' parents, however, were pretty cold toward me.

Besides Matson and Cooper, other guys in the house I remember as especially supportive and kind were Don Barnard, Dave Burpee, Gary Hoppes, Perry Koon, Dave Kopay, Jim Lagerquist, Ray Mansfield, John O'Brien, and Dave Phillips. Kopay, Mansfield, O'Brien, and Phillips played football for the

UW Huskies. Mansfield later played for the Pittsburgh Steelers on two Super Bowl winning teams in 1974 and 75.

I was the only Indian in the fraternity until a few years later when Sonny Sixkiller joined the house. He was the starting quarterback for the UW football team during 1970-72 and a full-blood Cherokee Indian who made the cover of *Sports Illustrated* in 1971.

Freshman year in college I stared out majoring in Business Administration. Being raised in poverty, this seemed logical to me at the time since I didn't want to ever be poor again. Like most Indians, however, I'm not a linear academic learner, so accounting, economics, and business law courses were a near disaster. Also, like most Indians, I'm an introvert, so marketing and Wall Street would have been out of the question. In addition, I resented being brain washed to worship the gods of profit and capitalism as taught in the UW Business School at that time. The pure capitalist ethos of "Greed is good" doesn't fit Indians too well.

Just by chance near the end of freshmen year, I was fortunate to overhear a couple students remark that Political Science was more interesting and easier than Business Administration. Since I was struggling academically at the time, this sounded pretty good. So I began taking Political Science courses my sophomore year and found it really interesting. I haven't regretted that choice.

Like most Political Science majors, my political views are strongly liberal. I also believed that unregulated capitalism as taught in the Business School didn't align well with Native cultural values of generosity and respect for the earth and other living things.

There was considerable stress those four years of college to avoid the military draft by always needing to work, while at the same time carrying a full academic load. Being drafted during those years meant I could be sent off somewhere in Southeast Asia to kill other brown people—or be killed or maimed myself. Unlike most rich white guys who could avoid the draft, most of us poor brown and Black citizens had little choice. There was no room for error if you didn't carry a full academic load, or had to drop out of college due to sickness or injury. Otherwise, it was hello Uncle Sam and off to a war that few of us in college supported, especially Political Science majors like me.

I couldn't have graduated from college in the summer of 1963 without the emotional and occasional financial support from my sister Marsha and my grandmother. They lived in another low-income housing project called Rainer Vista at that time and they provided a welcome place for me to come over from campus for dinners and laundry. Marsha also bailed me out a few times to make car payments on my 1954 Ford when I ran short of cash. Even today, she has always been the one to help out our extended family members, as well as many other relatives. Marsha is a strong and beautiful Native woman, a valued treasure in Indian Country who has kept our family together.

In high school I only got drunk about three times that I remember, but that was only because I didn't have the money or wasn't resourceful enough to get more booze. College was something else. Drinking was everywhere and I began to love the feeling of escape that alcohol instantly brought. It was magic, the medicine to cure my extreme introversion and to hide the social anxiety and fears as a half-breed Indian kid who grew up on welfare. College, therefore, became my first of five major drinking eras.

UW Sophomore Year (1960-61)
Marsha Spence Furfaro photo collection

Chapter 5
Kahuna and Moondoggie

Following my sophomore year at the University of Washington I experienced one of my most profoundly positive life changes—ocean lifeguarding on the Oregon coast at Seaside and surfing at Indian Beach.

How does a half-breed Indian kid from Montana become an ocean lifeguard at Seaside, Oregon? It began while walking by a job announcement board on the UW campus during spring term of my sophomore year. I happened to spot a small note about summer employment as a lifeguard at Cannon Beach, Oregon. Compared to the previous four summers working on horse racing tracks and in a plywood mill in Tillamook, this sounded pretty good. Fortunately, I'd just finished taking Senior Life Saving and Water Safety Instruction classes for Physical Education credit at the UW and I was eligible for a tryout.

I called the former Cannon Beach lifeguard who was giving tests at Greenlake Pool in north Seattle and he gave me a tryout. A couple days later he called to ask if I'd like to work at Seaside, Oregon since they had an opening there, and Cannon Beach was now fully staffed. I jumped at that offer, and as soon as college courses ended that spring of 1961 I drove down to Seaside in my old 1954 Ford for my first of three summers of ocean lifeguarding.

The first day at Seaside I found a small attic room in an old boarding house in town. A few days after starting to work on the beach, however, I was invited to share a house in Gearhart, Oregon with the Head Lifeguard, Steve Johnson. Steve was a football coach at Seaside High School and his roommate, Jim Ryder, was a track coach. They were two real personable and easy going older guys who also happened to be the most eligible bachelors in town. I was really fortunate to be accepted and to tag along for the ride with these two older guys who introduced me to the Seaside beach scene.

Lifeguarding at Seaside during the summers of 1961 and 62, and again in 1964 was nearly idyllic. It was a lot like *The Beach Boys* songs of that era—the ocean and surfing, beach fires and beach parties, the sun, and yes, the girls. Also, more importantly, for the first time I really experienced no prejudice from anyone for being an Indian with dark skin. I was judged solely on my ability as an ocean lifeguard. In 1962 and again in 1964 I was even asked to supervise the other guys as the Head Lifeguard. That gave me a huge boost in self-confidence that has been a life-changing experience.

We three lifeguards were supervised by the Chief of Police for the City of Seaside, and occasionally he allowed us to bring a fourth guard on duty if the beach was too crowded for safety. The fourth part-time lifeguard was an unforgettable beach character named Dick Rankin (aka "Kahuna").

Rankin was a University of Oregon student from Portland who had spent several summers in Seaside. He was a classic tanned blonde surfer who played guitar and drove an MG sports car. Rankin was the first to be invited to any beach party, or to start one himself. We soon became friends and he taught me how to play a ukulele to accompany his guitar. Folks started calling us "Salt and Pepper"—the blonde white guy and his dark skinned black-haired side kick.

Rankin, "Kahuna," had decided to call me "Moondoggie" that first summer lifeguarding in 1961. This was the nickname of a dark haired surfer in the old beach movie *Gidget* (1959). This is a handle that has stuck with me for a lot of our old beach friends all these years. Some beach friends and rugby teammates shortened it to "Dog" and later it was my name stenciled to an old jersey from playing with the original Jesters Rugby Club in Portland during 1974-76. One of my teammates on the Jesters also called me "Dog Soldier."

Other lifeguards with me in Seaside were Steve Johnson and Jim Zankich (1961); Roy "Hodun" Parnell and Gil Tolan (1962); David Grimes and Pete Henniger (1964). John Alto, Dave Davis, and Roy Parnell guarded in 1963 when I missed that summer to finish school at the UW. We had lots of rescues those four years and never lost anyone to drowning. I know all these other guys could also have some real interesting stories to tell.

The beach era included acceptance and affection shared with many folks who have remained lifelong friends, even if we have only seen each other occasionally. I have the fondest memories of John and Jerry Alto, Ace and Gary Anderson, Susie Burnham, Joe and Oney Camberg, Ralph and Betty Davis, Chuck Gilbert, Mark and Gary Hanson, Eddie Hendrickson, PK Hoffman, Kathy Kerwin, Peter Lindsey, Diane and Jackie McKee, Kathie O'Dell, Kathy Perrin, Dick Rankin, Jim and Jeff Roehm, Ky Weed, Norm Wilcox, the Grant girls, and many of the younger beach kids and surfers.

The only negative event during these three summers was the Seaside Riots during the 1962 Labor Day weekend. Lots of high school and college kids were in town for a concert by *The Wailers* and *Rockin' Robin Robbers*. When the concert was canceled, the kids were angry and this led to lots of drinking. They tore our lifeguard tower down and hauled it down Broadway where it was tipped over and it broke some young guy's leg.

The other lifeguards saw this happening, but there wasn't anything we could do to stop the crowd from this destruction. There was also a lot of damage to business storefronts and cars on

Broadway and many arrests were made for vandalism, fighting, and underage drinking. It became bad enough that the Seaside Police were overwhelmed and had to call for the National Guard to regain order.

The City finally helped quiet things down by paying for an outdoor concert on the beach. *The Wailers* performed on a roof outside of an underage nightclub called the Pypo Club which was just above the Turnaround at the beach on Broadway. Most of the rioters then ended up dancing and drinking on the beach and eventually everything settled down.

We had several surf rescues each summer and despite frequent late-night partying and hangovers, we never lost anyone to drowning during those four summers of 1961-64. We three lifeguards kept in shape running up and down the two miles of beach at Seaside almost every day and we swam out past the breakers for weekly drills every Thursday morning regardless of the weather and cold water.

We also learned to spot rip currents, to swim in them without panicking, and then practiced bringing each other back on shore. Rip currents were also just plain fun to ride—if a person understood not to fight against them and swim diagonally back to shore. We even used the rip current in the cove at the south end of the beach in Seaside to take us out past the breakers when surfing.

Besides rip currents that could frighten people and cause the inevitable signs of a panicked or distressed swimmer, most of our rescues happened during incoming tides involving sandbars. People would be jumping up and down in the waves on sandbars and then attempt to head back when they were tired or the waves got bigger. Due to the incoming tide, the slot between the sandbar and the beach becomes deeper and many swimmers don't account for that. When returning to shore, this slot would always be deeper than when a swimmer first went out. If this was over their head, or if a small rip was running out through the slot, this often caused a swimmer to panic and we were off to the rescue.

While we made lots of rescues and no one drowned those four summers, we had some real close calls. There were two particularly dangerous times that I vividly remember. On both occasions I carried a female swimmer back through the breakers who had swallowed seawater and was unconscious. In the first case, merely the rough action of running through the breakers while carrying the young lady back to the beach caused her to cough up some water and she was able to take some deep breathes again. She regained consciousness on shore and an ambulance quickly arrived to take her to the hospital where she fully recovered.

The second occasion was way more serious. I was in the lifeguard tower at the time and spotted through my binoculars a young lady and her boyfriend who had swum out beyond the breakers on the far north end of the beach. After observing them for a short while I could see they were in trouble. This was nearly a mile north of the lifeguard tower so it took a few minutes for the three of us to drive there and swim out to them. When I reached the young man he was totally exhausted while trying to hold up his unconscious girlfriend. In his panic he grabbed the buoy I was towing and let go of the girl. As she began to sink, I grabbed her wrist just in time and held her up until the other two guards arrived. We switched buoys and the other guards, David Grimes and Pete Henniger, were able to tow in the boyfriend with little difficulty.

Without the boy to worry about, I was then able to use a cross-chest carry to swim with the girl back through the breakers and then run with her through the shallow water. On shore I laid her down prone and used the back-pressure arm-lift method to push out some of the sea water she swallowed. She soon started some ragged breathing again, but hadn't fully regained consciousness before the ambulance arrived. We called the hospital later and were relieved to learn that she was all right and had no memory about most of the trauma she had experienced.

Other surf rescues weren't quite so dangerous. In fact, Dick Rankin and I shared one of the most fun experiences. It was an exceptionally warm sunny day and there was a big crowd at the beach so the Chief of Police authorized us to bring on Rankin. We saw that a number of people had been jumping up and down in the waves together on a long sandbar and they began to panic as the incoming tide created deeper water for them on their way in. Rankin and I decided to take out his surfboard since there were several people we needed to reach quickly and help keep them afloat. The other two guards took out buoys and were successful in swimming back with two of the individuals.

When Rankin and I reached the larger group, three or four people grabbed the surf board for dear life while we held on to the ends of the board and tried to help calm them down. Two other swimmers held onto two buoys attached to lines from our shoulder harnesses. This caused us all to be parallel to the waves and created more resistance for each wave to toss us around. Each wave would tumble us all over in every direction. Heads, arms, and legs were popping up all over the place in the white surf foam and it was a hilarious sight. Rankin and I knew we were all going to be okay and we barely kept from laughing at each other in the midst of it all. With the momentum of the waves and with all of us kicking and paddling we made it to shore and everyone was safe. Just another day at the beach.

Another rescue was even funnier and caused lots of laughter among the beach crowd. A pre-teen boy appeared to be having difficulty getting back to shore, and since there was a strong south drift that day I decided to take out the long line. This is a strong line attached to a large spool that could be used to reel us and the swimmers back in if the current was stronger than normal. The line is attached to a shoulder harness which I took out on this occasion.

While swimming out to the young boy, I felt quite a bit of resistance while towing the line through the breakers. Initially I thought the current must be way stronger than we had thought. When I turned to look back toward the line, however, I saw a foot sticking up in the water. It turned out that a drunken sailor had decided to help pull out the line from the spool and had somehow gotten himself tangled up—that was the resistance I felt. So I had to turn around to bring the sailor back to shore while the other guards reached the boy and towed him in with no problem. The young boy who was rescued was surprisingly calm and happy while the other guards brought him in. The drunk sailor was just fine once we returned to shore and we helped him cough up a bunch of seawater.

A reporter from the local weekly newspaper, the *Seaside Signal*, heard about this event that day and wrote this short article about it in the July 23, 1964 edition:

> Head Lifeguard John Spence appreciates help, but only when he looks for it. Last week he and the other guards went out to help a boy caught in the dangerous currents. They used the life line and while in the rescue operations a drunk decide to help.
>
> He became entangled in the line and sank. The guard brought both in and since the boy was alright they worked on the drunk, who was sobering up pretty fast. In the meantime, the boy left the scene and was never identified.

Later in that same edition of the paper, it noted that we rescued four other people that week. The week before on July 16 the paper reported that we brought in three people who needed help. I don't recall the numbers from my first two summers there, but I remember there were 16 people we rescued during my last year at Seaside in 1964.

The experience of lifeguarding at Seaside really helped me later in the summer of 1972 when I pulled up a young man from a deep pool on the Clackamas River at McIver State Park near Estacada, Oregon where my son, Erik, and I had gone fishing. The young man's friends were panicked and didn't know what to do. I dove down and found him in the deep water, brought him to the surface, and then used the back-pressure arm-lift method to get him breathing again. He didn't regain consciousness until after the fire and rescue folks showed up, but I found out later in a call to the hospital that he was fine except for a headache and didn't remember much about what had happened.

Dick Rankin and I became part of the lifeguard and surfing scene as told by Peter Lindsey in his book, *Comin' In Over the Rocks: A Storyteller's History of Cannon Beach* (2008, Saddle Mountain Press). Lindsey is a long-time Cannon Beach resident—a former teacher at Seaside, a lifeguard, and a Vietnam vet. In his book he provides an excellent account of the development of ocean lifeguarding and surfing on the northern Oregon coast.

Lindsey tells about a unique spot on the north part of Ecola State Park called Indian Beach. In his chapter on surfing, Lindsey describes it this way: "The hub of north coast surfing during its formative years was Indian Beach, a special place, a secret place, every surfer's dream." What an appropriate beach for this half-breed Indian to surf for the first time in 1962. John Alto, PK Hoffman, Dick Rankin, Jim Sagawa and lots of our other beach friends surfed there for several years during the 1960s and 70s following our lifeguard days.

Once in the summer of 1965, John Alto and I decided to paddle our surf boards from Indian Beach around Tillamook Head to Seaside. I don't recall which one of us thought up that crazy, dangerous idea. After about an hour battling the current and stronger winds in the open ocean off Tillamook Head, we gave up and headed back to Indian Beach. With the current in our favor and the strong tail wind, Alto and I made it back safely in no time. The adventures of youth can be pretty foolhardy.

Besides lifeguarding and surfing, the other major event from the beach years was meeting Diane. She was a University of Oregon coed and Miss Seaside of 1960. As an introvert who still didn't have a lot of self-confidence, it was a quite a struggle to get acquainted with her while she waited tables at her parents' restaurant near the beach in the summer of 1961. I drank gallons of coffee at her restaurant before working up the courage to ask her out for our first date. We went to Hug Point, a beautiful spot just south of Cannon Beach, ended up spending lots of time together, and were married after my second summer lifeguarding in 1962.

Unfortunately, the beach parties were over, my immaturity and drinking were too heavy at age 21, and the marriage ended two years later. When I returned to Seaside from two weeks of Marine Corps summer camp in 1964, I discovered that she had moved out of our apartment near the beach and went her own way.

With the exception of a failed first marriage, I look back fondly at the Seaside years as a hugely positive turning point in my life. For the first time I was given a major responsibility when I was asked to be the Head Lifeguard during my 2nd and 3rd summers. The funny thing about it was that it really wasn't surprising, it felt like a natural thing to do. Accepting the responsibility of Head Lifeguard was a totally new experience for me and greatly increased my self-confidence to approach future positions of responsibility and supervision.

A fun personal era ended after the summer of 1964. That September I began training as a caseworker for the Oregon Public Welfare Commission, and I've worked ever since in social work or human services positions, especially with tribes and Indian organizations.

Pete Henninger, me, David Grimes—last year lifeguarding (1964)
Photo from the Seaside Signal

Surfing and Rugby (1970)
Louise Lindsey photo collection

Chapter 6
Part-time Jarhead

During the summer term of my fourth year at the UW in 1963, I was living with Diane in a small apartment near campus. She was working in a bank and I was taking my final college classes while lifeguarding and teaching swimming classes at Echo Lake north of Seattle.

With graduation in August, I was now facing the military draft since my college deferment would end. The conflict in Vietnam had been heating up ever since the first US soldiers were killed there in 1959, and in 1963 US forces had been increased there to 15,000. My only options to avoid the draft and Vietnam were to either get a fake medical deferment (like Donald Trump), get arrested (like Mohammed Ali), flee to Canada (like some hippies), or to join a reserve or National Guard unit.

My friend Dick Rankin ("Kahuna") had finished college a year earlier than me, and to avoid the draft he joined the U.S. Marine Corps Reserves. He strongly advised me to forget the Marines, but I decided Rankin was wrong. He was always a little grandiose, and I figured the Marine Corps couldn't be as bad as he described it. Besides, Indian tribes have always been a warrior culture and that tradition played into my decision to join the Marines.

I figured the Marine Corps couldn't be as tough as their reputation. It was a challenge that I might as well try since I had a military service obligation with no way out. Also, World War II movies glorifying Marines fighting in the Pacific and a 1957 film called *The D.I.* (the Drill Instructor) made the Corps look interesting. *The D.I.* showed boot camp as really brutal and tough, but it also intrigued me. So I signed up for the U.S.M.C. Reserves based at Swan Island in Portland in September 1963 and flew off for boot camp near San Diego in October.

What a mistake! Rankin was right. Upon arrival we recruits were manhandled off the busses and roughly ordered to shut up while standing in several yellow footsteps painted on asphalt at the Marine Corps Recruit Depot (MCRD) near San Diego. We were subjected to the loudest, most extreme verbal abuse any of us had ever experienced. Drill instructors yelled and spit in our faces the most vile and creative profanities we had ever encountered.

This verbal abuse continued for all 13 weeks of boot camp in Platoon 382 at MCRD. We were also emotionally harassed and physically abused at other locations in the boonies of Camp Pendleton, on the Rifle Range at Camp Matthews, and finally in "C" Company at the Infantry Training Regiment (ITR).

Our hair had been completely shaved off and we were now "Jarhead" recruits—the lowest undisciplined scum in the eyes of the Marine Corps. Considered less than human by the drill instructors, we deserved no acceptance by the Corps until we could be "birthed through the bloody canal of boot camp" (Anthony Swofford in *Jarhead*, 2003, Scribner). Still today whenever I see the number of our platoon in boot camp I am jerked back to hearing the DIs screaming at us "382 . . . ON THE ROAD!" This always happened at zero dark thirty and my blood pressure would jump a few clicks.

The abuse wasn't just verbal and emotional. Our platoon of about 40 recruits were often punched in the stomach and throat by the DIs. Those were two places on the body where marks couldn't be left for the officers to see. I was also jabbed in both eyes once when a DI thought I was staring at him.

One recruit had his face bloodied by the fist of a drill instructor at ITR for some minor infraction. The recruit, a rugged white car clubber from California, was later encouraged by the same DI to fight a tough Black gang member from Chicago. It was a monumental bare-fisted fight that finally ended when the Black recruit got the white guy in a headlock, shoved his finger in the recruit's mouth, and ripped out a large gash that required several stitches.

Anthony Swofford in his powerful book, *Jarhead*, describes this kind of physical abuse in more detail than any other written account I have ever seen of Marine Corps life. On his second day of boot camp a DI slapped him on the back of the head a few times before slamming his head through a chalkboard into a cinder block wall. Another recruit in Swofford's platoon had a DI slam him hard in the chest with the butt of his rifle. Swofford's account of Jarhead life in peacetime and in combat during Desert Storm is a compelling story, brutally honest and profane, and probably difficult for the average American civilian to believe.

None of this physical abuse is allowed under the Uniform Code of Military Justice (UCMJ), but it's the Marine Corps way to turn us into some exceptional killers. None of us in Platoon 382 at boot camp or Company C at ITR formally protested this treatment. If we did, we could be charged with insubordination and sent to the brig for disobeying orders. Worse yet, a recruit could be declared a "slow learner" and set back in training indefinitely. That would be a three-month long groundhog day of living nightmares in boot camp.

There wasn't one word of positive reinforcement from the DIs, in boot camp or later. The Corps only believes in dispensing negative motivation and fear of the drill instructors and other NCOs (non-commissioned officers) so that orders are never disobeyed. I guess the cruel treatment in boot camp and ITR makes anything else look good, even combat.

During my six months of active duty in the Marines during October 1963 through March 1964, about half of our training platoon were reservists. We were constantly being harassed by the DIs to sign up for active duty. Apparently the DIs would be given cash incentives or some other kind of perks if they signed us up for active duty. After only a couple weeks in boot camp most of us reservists knew better than that. Four of us in the platoon were also college graduates and the DI's were really after us to enter officer candidate training. None of us four took the bait.

For my remaining five and a half years of reserve duty during 1964-69 the physical and verbal abuse wasn't quite as bad as the six months in boot camp and ITR. Physical tests, shooting weapons, blowing things up, forced marches, and war games were actually interesting at times. Bonding with other recruits during boot camp and in our reserve unit in Portland and at summer camps in California made it bearable. That and lots of beer and some epic drunken parties with others in my reserve unit. Heavy drinking in the Corps is accepted as long as you show up and the job gets done. Punishment is severe, however, if your drinking results in being AWOL or a hangover prevents you from being able to perform any assigned duties.

During my last year in the Marine reserves in 1968-69 there were over 500,000 US troops in Vietnam and our unit was put on 24-hour standby. We were ordered to have our sea bags packed and put by the door and report for duty immediately if called up.

At that time I was in my last year of grad school at Rutgers and had my second wife, Kris, and my son, Erik, with me. I worried about them if my unit was put on active duty, and I was definitely afraid of getting killed or wounded somewhere in Southeast Asia.

If called up to active duty I thought about getting into officer candidate school 1since I had a bachelors degree and had nearly completed a masters. Later, I was more than grateful for not being activated and for not taking officer training since it was revealed that the average lifespan of a Marine Corps 2nd Lieutenant in Vietnam was pretty short. In his book, *What It Is Like to Go to War* (2011), Karl Marlantes, a wounded and highly decorated Marine from Seaside, paints a pretty horrible picture of what my unit and I might have encountered in Vietnam.

Drinking in the Corps is tolerated, even celebrated, but my use of alcohol must have been pretty bad. While attending reserve meetings in Newark, New Jersey during 1968 I was "busted" (reduced in rank) from Lance Corporal to PFC (Private First Class). PFC is the second lowest enlisted rank. The platoon commander said my hair was too long, I was obviously hung over, and he didn't like the condition of my uniform. He ordered me to stand in front of our platoon, and he seemed to enjoy taking off my Lance Corporal stripes.

I think all Marine Corps veterans, if we're really honest about it, have a love/hate relationship with the Corps. As Anthony Swofford put it in *Jarhead*:

> The simple domesticity of the Marine Corps is seductive and dangerous. Some men claim to love the Corps more than they love their own mother or wife or children— this is because loving the Corps is uncomplicated. The Corps always waits for you. The Corps forgives your drunkenness and stupidity. The Corps encourages your brutality.

After completing my six-year Marine Corps reserves commitment in September, 1969, I never used to join the Indian veterans who were called up at pow wows for the grand entry. Since I'd only been a reservist who hadn't been in combat (and frankly, I wasn't a very gung ho Marine) I felt I didn't deserve to join the other Indian veterans. This changed one day after I'd returned to work in Montana for my tribe in 1980.

I'd become close to an Assiniboine (Nakoda) elder named Max White, a decorated World War II veteran and a highly respected traditional leader who took me as a nephew "in the Indian way." We were at a pow wow at the Fort Belknap Agency one time when Max asked why I hadn't joined with the veterans in the grand entry. I replied that I was only in the reserves and hadn't been in combat. Max, who was a wounded combat veteran in WWII, then asked if I would have gone to Vietnam if ordered to go. When I answered yes, he said that was ok then. He said I had been "holding the horses" as a reservist. Max said from now on I should join the other Indian veterans in grand entries at pow wows.

When a true Indian elder like Max White asks you to do something, you'd better do it. Max was the real deal, so now I join the veterans during grand entries at pow wows, help carry the flags when asked, and I attend the monthly Indian veterans meetings in Portland.

USMC boot camp graduation (January1964)
John Spence photo collection

Chapter 7
Client, Caseworker, and Grad Student

After my last day lifeguarding at the beach in Seaside on Labor Day 1964, I began training that September as a caseworker with the Clackamas County Public Welfare Department in Oregon City. This was an ironic change from my childhood as an ADC (Aid to Dependent Children) welfare client in Seattle. My two sisters and I used to hide from the welfare case workers since we heard they could take you away. This was in the years before the Indian Child Welfare Act of 1978 that provided protections for tribal children. The caseworkers often felt we'd be better off in white foster or adoptive homes. In those days our grandmother and uncle might not have been able to prevent our involuntary removal.

With this background, becoming a welfare caseworker wasn't a career goal I'd planned. It was just one of several job openings I'd seen posted in the Oregon state employment office that I could apply for with a bachelors degree. While considering this, I talked with a girl I knew from high school who was two years older than I and had begun work as a caseworker in California. She was the top scholar in her class and went on to graduate from Stanford. With her recommendation to check it out, that was good enough for me.

As it turned out, casework was interesting, challenging, and it's something I liked doing. Having grown up in poverty and on welfare myself, I identified with lots of the families on my caseload, and I could especially empathize with the kids. After two years working as a caseworker at Oregon City during 1964-66, I was fortunate to be awarded a stipend to go to graduate school for a Master of Social Work (MSW) degree.

Because of my Political Science background and interest in the Free Speech Movement at the University of California/Berkeley during 1964-65, Cal was my first choice for an MSW program. My application at Berkeley wasn't accepted, but I was approved for admission at Rutgers University in New Brunswick, New Jersey. Rutgers at that time was known as "Berkeley East" so I thought this could be interesting. Also, I'd never been farther east than North Dakota and thought this might be a good adventure.

Coincidently, a friend from beach days at Seaside, Terry Llewellyn, had to report to the army base at Fort Lee, Virginia about the same time that I needed to be at Rutgers. We drove out to the east coast together in separate cars, with a detour through Lake Tahoe for one last party with a friend who was working in a casino there. After we arrived at New Brunswick my friend Terry headed south to Virginia prior to shipping out to Vietnam.

My first week in New Brunswick in the fall of 1966 was a near disaster. I almost turned around to head back west. The east coast was an ugly place with air pollution, too many cars, and too many loud, rude people who wouldn't even acknowledge my presence when I asked directions. The first day in New Brunswick I came down with strep throat, and I had no place to stay. So I ended up driving around most of the night and finally sleeping in my car. The next day I was able to find a small depressing attic room near campus in an old house owned by a cranky, nosey landlady.

After joining the Marines, this looked like my second major mistake. While going to grad school at Rutgers, I also needed to attend monthly Marine Corps Reserves weekends at Newark, New Jersey—a place that was even more dirty and ugly than New Brunswick. Things weren't looking good on the East Coast for this half-breed Indian kid from Montana.

Grad school was toughest during my first semester of the two-year MSW program. All of us new grad students were stressed out and scared and the courses were tough. There was lots of racial diversity among students on campus, but little social justice course content in the School of Social Work, even though Rutgers had a very liberal reputation and lots of anti-war, civil rights, and welfare rights protests were going on then.

We grad students had a series of confrontations with the Dean of the School of Social Work to develop a more diverse curriculum, but he never budged. So we took matters into our own hands by community mobilizing with a local welfare rights organization. We ended up hosting some very lively welfare rights meetings right at the school, and having a good time doing it. This activity also promoted more bonding among us students, and our graduate school experience became less stressful during the second semester of my first year at Rutgers.

During that school year of 1966-67, opposition to the Vietnam war was heating up all over the country. Demonstrations against the war were being held on most college campuses, especially at Rutgers. After several of us grad students participated in anti-war demonstrations on campus, we decided to drive down to Washington DC to attend the March on the Pentagon there on October 21, 1967. I didn't have Marine Corps reserve duty that weekend so I was anxious to go to Washington with the other students.

It became the largest anti-war protest up to that point in 1967 with about 100,000 people. While attempting to reach the Pentagon, hundreds of citizens were beaten, tear gassed, and arrested by the National Guard and local police. Our student group was worried about getting expelled from graduate school so we chose not to cross the bridge to the Pentagon and were spared from the beatings and arrests like those who tried to cross.

As we were leaving the March, and after a few beers, I asked the other students I was with to drive me to the Bureau of Indian Affairs (BIA) building. When we stopped out front I walked up the stairs to the BIA and pissed on it. Yes, a crude gesture and my own little protest, but it felt good. I had always resented the paternalism by the BIA and the resulting tribal council impotence that this federal agency has perpetuated. Bureau employees on my reservation had better housing than the rest of us, more steady employment, and they often looked down on their less fortunate tribal members. Most Indians today still believe the BIA actually stands for "Boss Indians Around."

That first year at Rutgers became bearable as we students became better acquainted, more supportive of each other, and partied more together. Three of my fellow first year students became close friends—Bob Began from Boston, Larry Schwartz from Philadelphia, and Tom Moan from Eugene.

The other main thing that helped me survive at Rutgers was discovering the sport of rugby. I wound up playing both years on the Rutgers University team and drinking, of course, was a big part of the game.

At the end of that first year at Rutgers in 1967 I totaled my car when I passed out while driving home drunk from a grad school party on campus. An ambulance took me to the emergency room with a broken nose, facial cuts and bruises, and banged up knees. I somehow missed getting arrested for drunk driving and going to jail. Passing out while driving, totaling my car, and ending up in an emergency room should have reduced my heavy drinking, but it didn't. Unfortunately, it took several more years of drinking and totaling another car in 1974 before I finally sobered up at home in Montana in 1982.

In the summer of 1967 after that first year of grad school, I worked in Oregon City and continued seeing a University of Oregon coed, Kris, whom I'd known from lifeguarding days in Seaside. In January 1968 during my second year of grad school we got married before I returned to Rutgers after the winter break. Three months later our son Erik was born, and after graduation in June we drove back to Oregon. I then worked as a caseworker supervisor in Klamath County during 1968-69 while Kris finished school in Eugene.

Kris was the first person who confronted me with my drinking, but I wouldn't listen. My immaturity, dishonesty, and selfishness around drinking would doom this relationship two years later in 1970.

Chapter 8
Rugby is Life

One awful sleepless night during the fall of my first semester at Rutgers was the closest I ever came to a nervous breakdown. Adjusting to grad school was much tougher than I thought it would be. I hated the East Coast environment, and I didn't know anyone. I'm sure all of us MSW students initially experienced quite a lot of this same emotional suffering and loneliness. Most of us survived once we became better acquainted and adjusted to the tough academic schedule. The major reason for my own personal survival was discovering the sport of rugby.

While walking across campus one day I spotted a small note on a tree that read "IF YOU LIKE CONTACT AND YOU LIKE BEER, RUGBY IS THE GAME FOR YOU." That's an invitation I couldn't resist, so I took a chance one afternoon after class and checked out the team. A student from Hawaii named Steve Cook had been recruiting students and had just started the team at Rutgers that fall. Steve welcomed me and I soon joined the team for matches with other college and rugby club teams during each fall and spring of 1966-68.

Rugby is still a club sport (i.e., not a varsity team) on most college and university campuses and it hasn't yet been officially recognized by the National Collegiate Athletic Association

(NCAA) as an inter-collegiate or varsity sport. It's incredible growth in the U.S. might eventually lead to that, especially since rugby returned as an Olympic Sport in 2016 at the Rio Olympics.

Personally, I worry that the heavy-handed governance of the NCAA and their ruling moneyed interests might spoil the informal, inclusive culture of rugby. For example, as an MSW grad student I could play on the Rutgers University team during the two academic years of 1966-68. Later, I could also play on the University of Washington team as a PhD student for two more school years during 1976-78.

The world-wide informality and comradery of rugby might not be maintained under the strict rules of the NCAA. Beer is usually part of the sport when the home team hosts the visiting team after a match (this party is called "the 3rd half") and college rugby teams couldn't openly practice this if they were under the NCAA. It's the rugby club sides, however, where drinking after matches is much more common.

There was one very memorable home match with the Rutgers rugby team that I'll never forget. We played another team (I think it was the NY Rugby Club) on a large sports field on campus next to the football stadium where soccer, hurling (a rugged Irish sport), and lacrosse matches were also being played next to us. It was a beautiful day and some of our players had brought a keg of beer for the drink-up with the visiting team after the match. Our captain decided we'd carry the keg into the stadium stands to watch the football game. We somehow managed to carry that keg in without anyone stopping us and both teams drank it during the Rutgers football game. I don't know if a group of rowdy, dirty, sweaty rugby players with a keg of beer has ever been allowed back in that stadium, or if a similar event has ever happened on another college campus. It was a singular memory from 12 years of playing rugby during 1966-78.

After graduating from Rutgers in June 1968 I returned to Oregon to work for one year in Klamath Falls for the Klamath County Public Welfare Office. That year I hooked up with the Portland Rugby Club ("The Pigs") and played there from 1968-73. There was really no formal election and I didn't ask for it, but the boys drafted me as the Portland Rugby Club President in 1969 and for three more years through 1972.

The Portland guys who put me in that leadership position were 30 or more pretty rough and socially irreverent characters. Along with being chosen Head Lifeguard at Seaside, being President of the Portland Rugby Club was an honor that I still find hard to believe could happen for an introverted half-breed Indian like me. Like the beach era when I was asked to be the Head Lifeguard, beer and partying helped overcome my social awkwardness to handle the responsibility as rugby club president.

Around 1971 more Oregon State University and University of Oregon players joined the club after graduating, and The Portland Pigs became a pretty competitive club. With our winning records we then qualified for the Monterey National Rugby Tournament in 1972 and 1973. We won two matches and lost two both years at Monterey. At one of the tournaments some friends even hauled down our mascot to the tournament—"Gladys," a very large female pig.

Some guys I remember from playing with the Pigs during 1968-73 were Barry Best, Dave Bottemiller, Ron Cronin, Jim Davis, Frank Dierickx, Denny Freed, Harvey Hetfield, Jim Gidley, Herb Howell, Tom Hussey, Russ Lynde, Bill Martindale, Vince McGarry, Dan Myers, Joe Phillips, Bill Ranta, Greg Robbins, Rob Reynolds, Dick Scafford, Jon Sutcliffe, Michael Sweeney, Keith Swensen, and Terry Vulcani. There were lots of others, I just can't remember all the names after over 40 plus years.

There was only one other Indian guy who played with me on the Pigs and Jesters rugby clubs, Bruce Butterfield (Chippewa

Cree). We occasionally still get together to watch the hard-fought annual rivalry matches between the Pigs and the Jesters (now called ORSU—the Oregon Rugby Sports Union).

Due to the demands of working with The War on Poverty program in Portland during 1970-72, and then the Indian Social Work Education Project at Portland State University from 1972-76, I tried to retire from rugby in 1973. That wasn't to be. A group of young PSU rugby players showed up at my office one day and said they wanted me to be their player-coach. I couldn't resist the invitation from these kids, so I wound up as their player-coach at PSU during the 1973-74 school year. These students were fast and tough and eager to learn. For a new team we did really well immediately by winning way more than half of our matches. We also competed at the Golden Gate Rugby Tournament in San Francisco and The Mud Ball Rugby Tournament in Seattle.

At the end of that school year the PSU Athletic Department cut off our traveling budget. One of the reasons besides cutting athletic department costs was that some beer cans were found in a university van after our San Francisco trip. The PSU students and I were then asked to join up with a bunch of older players from the Portland Rugby Club in 1974 to form a new team in Portland called The Jesters. The Portland Rugby Club had really grown with the addition of more OSU and U of O grads, so this was a perfect time for the sport of rugby to expand in our area.

The idea for forming The Jesters by including a bunch of older ruggers from the Pigs and inviting the younger PSU players to join them was a plan hatched by Jon "The Troll" Meads and David "Botts" Bottemiller. These two characters were very experienced, charismatic, fearless old rough necks who were the main founders in contributing to the success that the Jesters enjoy today. Original Jesters from 1974 who I can remember were Barber, Botts, Burba, Cleveland Ray, Cronin, Davis, Dego, Dog, Gano, Harvey, Dan and Roy Lucas, PC, Pigpen, Rowan,

Ruble, Ruchek, Saul, Scafford, Simmons, Still, Troll, Wee Willie, and Yak. There were some others whose names escape me right now.

With the speed and strength of the younger PSU players and the toughness and experience of the former Pigs players, the new Jesters immediately became a very competitive rugby team that has grown and flourished ever since. I played with the Jesters the first two years of the club from 1974-76 before leaving for a doctoral program at the University of Washington in the fall of 1976. A few years later The Jesters were renamed ORSU (the Oregon Rugby Sports Union).

During 1976-78 I played my last two years of full-time Division I rugby at the UW. Our coach was a very experienced rugger named Rick Ristau who was on the mend from several injuries while he played with the Old Puget Sound Beach Rugby Club. Another experienced older player from the East Coast named Fred Meyer also joined us at that time. With the three of us experienced older guys and a bunch of fast, tough, young players we immediately became successful and were invited to the Monterey National Rugby Tournament in the spring of 1977 and again in 1978. At Monterey each year we won two matches and lost two.

On the UW Rugby Team there was one other Indian student besides me. Don Motanic (Coeur d'Alene/Umatilla) later returned to Yakima and started a local rugby team there. Don is a long-time tribal timber manager who has worked successfully to preserve and restore natural resources with northwest tribal governments. He has also been very active over the years to help recruit and support tribal students into the American Indian Science and Engineering Society (AISES).

After the UW rugby club returned from the Monterey Tournament that first year in 1977, the team had our end of the year party on Camano Island. While there the boys surprised me with a plaque as the Inspirational Player for 1976-77, an honor I'll never forget.

I was really fortunate to end my full-time rugby days on a high note with the UW team that last year in 1977-78. The years of rugby, and later rodeo, were taking a physical toll on me, but being able to play first team rugby my last two years with the boys on the UW Team was a memory I'll always cherish.

Some of the UW ruggers I recall were Bill "Wheels", Doug Bouchet, Chub, Chucky, Doctor, Sid Eland, Larry Henchy, Jim Janke, Rob Leroy, Malcom, Dan and Terry McTaggart, Bill McLoughlin, Don Motanic, Fred Myer, Jerry Polley. John Watters, and Scotty Williams. There were many others whose names escape me, but I just remember this whole team as being a real quality bunch of young guys without an ounce of racism.

The personal inclusion and absence of racism I discovered in rugby was a tremendous attraction for me. This is an aspect of the sport, in addition to the camaraderie and physicality, that kept me playing for 12 years and continues to hold much affection for me.

Since 1978 I've only played in a few "Old Boys" rugby matches. These are very informal games with a bunch of former players over 40 who don't practice and just get together occasionally for the comradery, and the excuse to drink beer away from wives and kids. For a lot of us the sport of rugby is too addictive to let go completely.

The Portland Rugby Club Pigs began in 1961, the Jesters in 1974, and now there are two newer men's teams in Portland called the Eastside Tsunami and the Portland Lumberjacks. Portland area rugby teams compete well in regional and national tournaments and often send players to the national team—the USA Eagles. Women's rugby is also well established in Portland.

The Lady Jesters won the national Division I championship in 2014—the highest level of rugby in the country. A few Lady Jesters have even been selected to the USA Eagles national team.

Rugby has a fall and spring season and I was lucky enough to play every year from 1966-78. The only half-season I missed was the fall of 1975. I needed that time to heal up from a broken arm dealt me by a bull named Avenger in the All-Indian Rodeo at Fort Hall, Idaho in August of that year.

Rugby teams are generally welcoming to anyone who can handle the physical nature of the game and can contribute to the comradery and culture of a particular rugby club. Players often change club teams to fit their own personalities and skills. After competing in high school or college rugby, players grow to love the game so much that they can't face life without it. Club sides and Old Boy tournaments can provide life-long friendships and allegiances.

A common saying in the rugby world is "Rugby is Life" and there's a lot of truth to that. Drinking, truth be told, is a big part of rugby, and my truth is that I over did it way too many times. My second wife Kris was especially critical of my drinking with the Portland Pigs rugby team.

With my low self-esteem, I had always needed alcohol to feel accepted in most social situations, and even with rugby I often took it too far. After college, lifeguarding, and the Marines—rugby was my fourth major drinking era. It was during the rugby era that my wife Kris really got after me for drinking too much. I wouldn't slow down in my partying and drinking and we divorced in 1970. It would still be a few more years, however, that I finally got honest with myself and others to sober up back home at Fort Belknap, Montana in 1982.

UW Rugby vs. Skagit Valley (1977)
Rob Leroy photo collection

UW Rugby Team (1976-77)
Rob Leroy photo collection

Chapter 9
Part I: The 1970s—Indian Activism, Guerilla Social Work, and Indian Poets

The 1970s for the country began with lots of positive momentum from the Civil Rights and Black Power movements of the 1960s. In 1968 there had been some tragic setbacks. Besides growing opposition to the Vietnam War, there was the assassination of Martin Luther King on April 4, 1968, and then the next month Bobby Kennedy was shot and killed on June 5th. This was followed by the Democratic National Convention in Chicago in August where the police beat, gassed and arrested hundreds of young people. And then Richard "Tricky Dick" Nixon was elected president on November 5, 1968.

With two more years of Nixon escalating the Vietnam War, events in the spring of 1970 took an even more ugly turn for the country. On May 4, 1970 at Kent State University the Ohio National Guard opened fire on unarmed white college students and others who were protesting Nixon's decision to widen the war by bombing Cambodia. The Guard killed four students and wounded nine others, including one who suffered permanent paralysis. Then on May 15, 1970, city and state policemen shot and killed two unarmed Black students who were protesting the war at Jackson State University and 12 others were wounded.

Still, Vietnam would drag on for five more years until the fall of Saigon on April 30, 1975.

These events really impacted me, and they contributed to my personal commitment and political activism over the course of my life. The tragic deaths of Dr. King, Bobby Kennedy, and the students at Kent State and Jackson State in 1968 affected me deeply. This led to my activism and social justice work and the way I viewed the world and helped me immensely when I finally sobered up and quit drinking.

Lots of us in Indian Country became particularly empowered during the 1960s and 70s. A lot of the current activism with tribes and urban Indian communities began with the "Fish-Ins" and "Fish Wars" of the 1960s and 70s in the Puget Sound area in Washington. Puyallup tribal members like Robert Satiacum, Ramona Bennett, and others were beaten and arrested while asserting their treaty rights to fishing on the Puyallup River. News coverage of this led to the active involvement of actor Marlon Brando, and he was arrested in 1964 while fishing with Bob Satiacum on the Puyallup River. Comedian and long-time civil rights activist Dick Gregory was arrested in 1966 while supporting Billy Frank, Jr. (who was arrested over 50 times) for fishing on the Nisqually River.

The Fish Wars of the 1960s-70s highlighted for America the general state of human rights abuses and poverty among Indians and neglect of treaty rights by the federal and state governments. These events led to the Boldt Decision of 1974 where it was declared that federally recognized tribes held treaty rights to half the harvestable salmon. Even with this legal decision, however, salmon numbers in the Northwest have continued to decline due to river water shortages, failure to eliminate harmful dams, excessive non-Indian commercial fishing, and habitat degradation due to over-harvesting of timber and clear cuts.

Besides the Fish Wars, the Occupation of Alcatraz by Indians in 1969 really got things going and seemed to rally Indigenous folks everywhere in Indian Country. Alcatraz was followed by the takeover of Fort Lawton in Seattle by Bernie White Bear, Randy Lewis, Ramona Bennett, and other Indian activists around Seattle in 1970. Then there was the occupation of the BIA in Washington, DC by the American Indian Movement (AIM) in 1972. I participated in both the takeover of the local Portland, Oregon BIA office and the occupation of Camp Adair near Corvallis in 1972. In 1973 AIM occupied Wounded Knee and then there was the Longest Walk in 1978 from San Francisco to Washington, DC.

While the Boldt Decision of 1974 was supposed to guarantee NW tribes the right to an equal share of the salmon harvest for sustenance and cultural ceremonies, their declining numbers and failure to protect tribal fishing rights led to a long-time personal protest by David Sohappy (Yakima) and his family. He and his relative Richard Sohappy were first arrested in 1968 for fishing at Cooks Landing where they lived on the Columbia River. The Sohappy family kept fishing at their home site while harassment from state law enforcement agencies and white sport fishermen continued. David and his son David, Jr. and several others were arrested in 1982. David Sr. was sentenced to five years and imprisoned from 1983-85. He was released early due mainly to the intervention of U.S. Senator Daniel Inouye from Hawaii.

Documentation of Portland urban Indian community organizing and activism during the 1950s through current times will be available soon in a book titled *Round Dance* by Dr. Claudia Long (Nez Perce). Dr. Long has interviewed and recorded the recollections of dozens of us local Natives who were involved during this time.

My personal involvement during the decade of the 70s began by being asked to leave employment with the Oregon State Public

Welfare Commission in Salem in July 1970. The agency leadership was upset that some of us younger casework supervisors were allowing welfare rights and farm workers meetings to be held in the basement of the Marion County Welfare office where I was working during 1969-70.

These were really lively and fun meetings, especially since La Raza and the Chicano and Farm Workers Movements were in full swing in Marion County. I remember Frank Martinez was a very eloquent speaker in our area who mobilized lots of the farm workers to organize and take action. I also recall Maria Benevidez, who worked with me at the Marion County Welfare Office, as the main organizer for local welfare rights organizing.

The Director of the Oregon Public Welfare Commission, Andrew Juras, then began getting political pressure from his more conservative upper level agency staff about allowing these meetings in our office. I'm not completely sure why I was the only casework supervisor singled out for hosting these meetings, but Mr. Juras offered to let me out of the last year of my employment commitment if I resigned, or else I'd just be fired. At that time I still owed the agency one more year of work due to their graduate school stipend awarded to me for the MSW program at Rutgers University during 1966-68. I wasn't exactly fired, but I was the only casework supervisor asked to resign.

To tell the truth, I was relieved to leave the rigid structure of that state agency in July 1970, and I looked forward to a potential job offer with the War on Poverty Program in Portland. Mr. Juras was actually quite gracious about asking me to leave and it didn't feel exactly like being fired.

Prior to my leaving the agency, some of the other Marion County Welfare Commission staff and I had also been asked by the local welfare rights and farm workers groups to assist with planning a statewide "Poor Peoples Conference" to be held in October 1970 at the State Fairgrounds in Salem. Because of my involvement in this effort, some staff members at the local War on Poverty program—the Portland Metropolitan Steering Committee (PMSC)—encouraged me to apply for a new position at their office.

That position was to work with a new low-income substance abuse program that had just been funded by the federal Office of Economic Opportunity earlier in the summer of 1970 called the Alcoholism Counseling and Recovery Program (ACRP). An MSW level project director was preferred for the position and it was perfect timing since I'd just been forced out at the Oregon Public Welfare Commission at the end of June.

An interview committee for the position met with me in July 1970. The committee consisted of a Black agency staff administrator, Marcus Glen, and four ACRP counselors who had just been hired. The counselors were all recovering alcoholics with long-time sobriety. They were a formidable bunch of street-wise characters who really believed in the "tough love" approach to recovery. I remember at the end of the interview that Mr. Glen said, "I like John" and he recommended that I start work the next month in August.

The four counselors included a full-blood Modoc Indian from the Klamath Tribes in southern Oregon named "Big Al" Smith and his long-time buddy in sobriety, a Chicano named "Sweet Luis" Polanco. Al and Luis had done time in San Quentin and sobered up together there. Another of the original counselors was Emile Summers—a tall, very impressive Black guy from Deadwood, South Dakota. The ACRP counselors called Emile "The Midnight Cowboy" because he was from Deadwood and always wore a classic black cowboy hat and shiny black cowboy boots. The other full-time counselor was a white guy named Casey Jones, a former WWII pilot who had flown many missions "over the hump" from India to China during the war.

These were four tough older guys who you wouldn't want to tangle with in a bar fight. They really had me sweating during the interview, but they decided they'd give me a chance since the agency wanted an MSW and a person of color for a director position. It's ironic that at the time I was still trying to be "just a social drinker," who wasn't ready to confront my own dependence on alcohol.

We also hired a beautiful red-headed receptionist, Myra, who was mostly sober (and whom I later learned had been dating both Al and Luis during this time). The agency then let us hire some counselor trainees and we were off and running in August 1970. Other programs around town soon began calling us "The Dirty Dozen." We didn't care, in fact, we liked it. This was the most personally powerful, creative, and fearless group of service providers I've ever known.

The ACRP counselors weren't afraid of anything and they were the most tireless advocates for their clients that I've ever seen. They would take turns going into the Portland City Jail almost every morning since in those days public intoxication was still a crime. The presiding judge would usually take their recommendations on what to do with some sad or boisterous drunk who'd been picked up on Burnside the night before.

With their tough love approach, the ACRP counselors told a potential client that if he or she could walk the one mile from the jail to our office, we would help them sober up. I often looked out our second story window and witnessed some poor soul barely shuffling uphill from the city jail to the ACRP office on SE 11th and Morrison. Only then would the counselors do a formal intake.

The counselors also did a lot of outreach on the skid row streets around West Burnside and up at "pill hill" (Oregon Health Sciences Hospital and the V.A. Hospital) and at other hospitals in the Portland area. Their "12 Step Calls" in parks and shelters around town also kept the counselors on the run days, nights and weekends, and they often took me along with them. These guys were tireless and had a lot of fun in their work. I learned a lot from these rough characters about "guerilla social work"— unconventional actions from the heart and fearless advocacy for the poor.

During that summer of 1970 the ACRP counselors also began functioning as the unpaid staff for the Native American Rehabilitation Association (NARA)—an Indian treatment program in Portland that was started earlier that spring by a Menominee Indian named Steve Askenette. Steve had recently been released from the Oregon State Penitentiary and was the consummate ex-con hustler. He guilted and conned the Council of Churches and other service agencies to pay rent for the first NARA house at NW 24th and Quimby in Portland.

Steve asked the ACRP counselors to provide most of the direct service work for the first two years for NARA clients during 1970-72. Al Smith and his friend John "Buzz" Nelson (Lakota) and I also joined the NARA board of directors that summer. Buzz, an impressive Indian guy from South Dakota is a Marine and a Korean War veteran who is the longest serving board member, volunteer, mentor, and champion for the NARA program. A few years ago he was awarded a plaque for being "The NARA Guy."

NARA clients also pitched in to hustle for furniture and pooled their food stamps to keep things going. With a lot of support from the local Indian AA group, the Native community, and the local AIM chapter, NARA kept afloat without any funding for the first two years of the program. Then in 1972 a state worker and I were asked to write the first federal funding grant for the program. We were all elated when after two years of operating without any funding NARA could finally hire a paid full-time staff of counselors.

Since then, especially due to great leadership from Dr. Sidney Stone Brown (Blackfeet) during the 1980s and Dr. Gary Braden (Ojibwa) during the 1990s, both federal and state grant funding have grown immensely. Jackie Mercer has directed NARA for the past 20 years and it is now a multi-million dollar comprehensive health, wellness, and substance abuse prevention and treatment program.

In 1970 I met one of my closest and long-term friends, Ed Edmo (Shoshone/Bannock). Ed has since become a very well-known poet, teacher, and playwright. He and I still attend lots of Indian AA meetings together and we always cap off evenings with "donut therapy." Most of us recovering alcoholics have an insatiable sweet tooth, so Ed and I have our own little ritual with donuts at the end of meetings or some other Indian community activity. Ed and I joined the original AIM chapter in Portland to occupy the Portland Area Office of the BIA in 1972, and then we occupied an abandoned military base called Camp Adair, also in 1972. In 1973 Ed also took part in the takeover at Wounded Knee, South Dakota.

Edmo has two colorful rap sheets from the Portland Police and the FBI that we always really get a kick out of due to the official cop language that describes Ed's activities and his alleged propensity for violence. From an FBI report written on July 6, 1973:

> ED EDMO, American Indian believed to be from Ft. Hall, Idaho Indian reservation. He is a member of the Portland AIM who may present a problem . . . He has repeatedly made statements that he has thoughts of barricading himself in a building and shooting as many white persons as possible.

Ed and I always laugh about this whenever we get together. He has been an invited speaker to my social work classes at Portland State University and has only missed one class in 20 years. During class Ed liked to read the above excerpt from his rap sheets. The graduate students in my class always appreciated hearing from a real authentic Indian activist and guerilla social worker like Edmo.

During 1971-72 the ACRP counselors and clients also occupied three houses in Portland to gain more halfway houses for low-income clients. The first one was a city-owned house at SE 20th and Taylor in Portland that another poverty program had vacated. In the spring of 1971 the ACRP counselors moved their clients into the house without asking permission from the City of Portland. I knew ahead of time they planned to do this, and as the program director I was worried that the counselors and I might get arrested for such a crazy guerilla action.

The counselors then came up with a scheme to keep their clients from getting evicted, and maybe keep our ACRP staff and me from getting arrested for trespassing. They decided to invite the Mayor of Portland to have dinner at the house and hear directly from the clients how this place and our program were helping them get sober and gain self-sufficiency. The Mayor, Neil Goldschmidt, was so impressed by the clients that he persuaded the City Council to pass an ordinance to allow our clients to stay there rent-free for six months and waive the building codes. At the end of this six months period we packed City Hall with lots of clients and community supporters for the next hearing on this action. This resulted in another six-month rent-free extension from the City. In the meantime, the ACRP counselors formed a non-profit organization called Harmony House and the clients somehow found ways to keep things going by selling blood, part-time day labor, and pooling their food stamps.

Emile Summers, an ACRP counselor who was highly regarded in the Black community, approached us one day while this was going on to tell us he'd found a house that his Black clients could occupy. Apparently, a militant Black Power group (not the Black Panthers) had seized a house in north Portland owned by Emmanuel Hospital. This group told us they'd found another house and to just move in Emile's Black clients and let them deal with the hospital. No problem. Emmanuel Hospital was more than willing to have our clients live in the house instead of the Black Power group. This became the second Harmony House, and the name was later changed to Freedom House.

Also during this time, one of our female counselor trainees named Peggy decided that her female clients needed a house too. I don't remember who owned this place in NE Portland, but it soon became another Harmony House, but for women only. Years later one of the original Dirty Dozen, Russell Duke, said during a recent visit with Ed Edmo and me, "ACRP and Harmony House . . . there was just no way that these programs should have worked, but they did."

After working at ACRP for two years I went to work at Portland State University for their new Indian Education Project at the School of Social Work in 1972. Leaving ACRP wasn't easy. The Dirty Dozen were some unique humans—courageous and tough characters who were true fighters in The War on Poverty. Most of us have remained life-long friends. I'll never forget them.

The other two Indian Education project staff at the PSU School of Social Work during our first year together were Emma Gross, MSW (a super bright, fun-loving lady from Puerto Rico) and Etta Conner (Umatilla), a tough Indian cowgirl. The second year of the program we were able to add Tom Jones (Lummi/Siletz). During our years together the three of us recruited over 50 full-time Indian students into the graduate and undergraduate social work education programs at PSU, as well as into a two-year social services associate degree program in human services at Portland Community College.

Emma and I also developed and taught tribal specific social work courses during the first four years of the project. I then left for a doctoral program at the University of Washington in the fall of 1976. Emma also left at the same time for a doctoral program at the University of Utah. The Indian Social Work Education project lasted for ten years through two 5-year funding grants from the National Institute for Mental Health (NIMH).

I'd only been on the job at PSU a couple of weeks when some of our Social Work project students and other Indian students took over the PSU President's office. They had been sharing a small office in the Multi-Cultural Student Center at PSU and felt they needed their own space. This occupation also worked. The students were successful in getting their own small office, and a few years later a separate Native American Student and Community Center was built.

Later during my first academic year at PSU in 1972-73 some other Indian students occupied the President's office again. This was a group of 14 Blackfeet Indian freshmen from Browning, Montana who had been recruited by a Teacher Corps staff member, Sidney Stone, a PSU graduate. These Blackfeet students' financial aid was late and they had no place to stay. PSU administrative staff quickly found a large house in NE Portland for the students to stay and speeded up their financial aid grants. The students named their house "The Great Spirit Indian Lodge". Unfortunately, homesickness and drinking got the best of these students and only one finished the school year at PSU.

Besides Ed Edmo, I became acquainted with three other Indian poets during the 1970s who have since made their mark both locally and nationally.

I met Vince "Spook" Wannassay (Cayuse/Umatilla), an Indian poet, artist, activist, and community organizer in the early 1970s. His brother, Tino, was already a student in our Indian social work program, and he was trying to recruit Spook to PSU. Tino actually plagiarized a PSU application for his brother and informed Spook one day that he was now a college student—you could get away with things like that at the time.

When he got his first student financial aid check Spook told me he was "Indian rich," although he and Tino were still living on food stamps. While he and Tino were going to school at PSU they were sharing rent with another Indian student, Pete, who had just been released from the Oregon State Penitentiary. They were surprised one day when city cops burst into their apartment. It seems that Pete had been robbing banks near PSU, and a whole bunch of cash was found hidden in his room in their apartment. Spook used to like to tell that story to my social work classes at PSU.

Spook sobered up and went on to represent the Portland Indian community in more non-profit boards and public agencies than anyone else. He became one of the most talented and well-respected Native leaders in Portland and the region. His going home ceremony in 2017 was attended by hundreds of people, both Indian and non-Indian as well.

A younger Indian poet was also developing her talents during this Indian activist period of the 1970s in Portland. Elizabeth "Lizzie" Woody (Navajo/Warm Springs/Wasco/Yakama) is the daughter of one of our most well-known Indian substance abuse counselors and AIM activists in Oregon, Charlotte "Sugar" Pitt. Sugar's place in Portland was the designated AIM house during the 1970s. Lizzie and her younger sister Joey took part as kids in lots of Indian activism and community organizing during this time.

Lizzie has continued her mother's legacy of activism and has taught creative writing at the Institute of American Indian Art (IAIA) in Santa Fe. She has also worked at Ecotrust in Portland and completed a Masters in Public Administration from the Hatfield School of Government at PSU. Her published poetry has won lots of awards and is widely recognized for its power and beauty in describing her homeland and imparting cultural knowledge. Lizzie has contributed to an Indigenous sage brush rebellion that burns up the plateau. As a result, she was selected as the Oregon Poet Laureate for 2016-18 and is now the Museum Director at her home, the Confederated Tribes of Warm Springs.

The fourth Indian poet I met during the 1970s was Henry "Hank" Real Bird (Crow). Hank and I actually met while riding in Indian rodeos during the 1970s. We shared rent in an apartment in Portland for a few months during the 1975-76 academic year when both of our girlfriends had kicked us out after a summer of rodeoing together in 1975.

Riding broncs and ranching might have been Hank's first loves, but he became well-known as a teacher, writer of children's books, and an award-winning Indian cowboy poet. He was selected as the Montana Poet Laureate for 2009-11 and during that time he rode horseback through most of Eastern and Northern Montana handing out books of his poetry in many of the small prairie towns on his trail. "The approach was so unusual that it made national news. Real Bird was interviewed twice on NPR, and was invited to speak around the country." ("The Bard of the Bighorn," Montana State University, October 13, 2014)

The early 1970s were impactful in so many ways. Even though my dependence on alcohol was mostly hidden with Indian community activism, The Dirty Dozen, the PSU Indian students, and the Indian poets, memories and friends from this time are all so dear to me.

The Dirty Dozen (1970-72)
Top: Pat Salsbury, "Big Al" Smith, "Sweet Luis" Polanco,
Emile "The Midnight Cowboy" Summers, Casey Jones,
Dave Davis, Russell Duke
Bottom: John Koerner, Myra Albert, Glen Yeats, John Spence, Ben Wright
John Spence photo collection

Chapter 10
Part II: The 1970s—Indian Rodeo, Indian Basketball, Teepee Creeping, and a Doctoral Program

Besides a lot of interesting and often stressful work and community activities during the 1970s, I look back on that time with a lot of good memories related to sports, friends, guerilla social work, and completing course work at the University of Washington in a PhD program. While great times continued with playing rugby during 1966 through 1978, I was also able to finally dive into another passion in 1973—Indian rodeo.

Rodeo has a strong hold on a lot of us in the west, but All-Indian Rodeo is something special. Rodeo has roots in ranch work, and it's only natural that skills like calf roping, steer wrestling, and riding wild horses and bulls would evolve into a competitive sport. While rodeo has a long history in the US, it's only in about the past 60 years that Indian rodeo really took off as a sub-culture of the sport.

There isn't any mystery why All-Indian rodeo started and why it is so popular now on most reservations in the west. A lot of white farmers, ranchers, and cowboys involved with rodeo can be real rednecks, or outright racist. When Indians compete in open or professional rodeos against white cowboys, they are often given lower scores and can be subject to disrespect and discrimination.

In All-Indian Rodeo, however, there is a comfort, comradery, and lack of stress quite different than other rodeos. Unlike most rodeo competitors, I didn't have a dad, uncle, or older brother around to help get me started in the sport. I'd had a long-time fascination with Indian rodeo, but playing rugby and working full-time kept me from fully getting into it. Finally, in 1973 at 32 years of age I decided to give it a try.

A friend named Charlie Scott had started riding bareback horses and bulls and he encouraged me to try it. Charlie is an Alaskan Native, a Marine, and a downhill ski racer. He is one tough hombre and the most outgoing and fun-loving character of any of our many rodeo pals. Even at white rodeos if you see or hear a bunch of cowboys laughing and horsing around, it's going to be Charlie as the instigator and the guy with the loudest laugh.

Charlie loaned me his bareback rigging for my first ride on a bucking horse in an All-Indian Rodeo. This rodeo was held at the He He Campground on the Warm Springs Indian Reservation in Oregon in 1973. I was pretty nervous and the horse bucked me off, but I was hooked. That first year Charlie and I travelled to several rodeos around Oregon and Washington, and that summer I rode a bareback horse at home at the little Lodge Pole Rodeo at Fort Belknap.

In the spring of 1974 I rode my first bull at an indoor practice arena near Sandy, Oregon. Pete LaMere, a Chipewa Cree cowboy from the Rocky Boy Reservation in Montana, loaned me his bull rope and provided some instruction as I sat down on my first bull in the bucking chute. Fear, yes, everyone has it in different degrees while riding bulls (more so than riding bucking horses), but the crazy fun outweighs it.

That summer I rode a bull at the Rodeo Drive arena at home at Fort Belknap. At the rodeo the handle on my bull rope broke off, and it's a pretty strange experience sitting on a bull with nothing to hold on to. The rodeo announcer, Joe Brown, gave me a little grief for not checking my gear, but it was worth a few laughs. Later that summer in 1974, Charley Scott and I entered the big Crow Fair and All-Indian Rodeo at Crow Agency, Montana. Charley bucked off his bareback horse and my bull threw me around pretty good. So naturally that night we had to drown our sorrows with our old rodeo buddy, Hank Real Bird, at the infamous Hilltop Bar in Hardin, Montana. The Hilltop was one of the toughest Indian cowboy bars around with lots of fights and shootings, but it has since burned down.

Charlie Scott and I also competed as a team in the wild horse race event at several rodeos. This event involves a team of three guys trying to saddle a wild horse so one of them can mount and ride the horse across a finish line without getting bucked off. Several other teams are in the rodeo arena trying to do the same thing and the first horse and rider across the finish lines wins. It can be a pretty wild and crazy scene. I only took first in two rodeo events and both were in the wild horse race. Charlie, Oly Meanus (Warm Springs), and I won at the Tygh Valley, Oregon All-India Rodeo in 1975. Then in 1977 Charlie, Patrick Melendey (Hoopa), and I won at Molalla, Oregon. Charlie, Ray Mayfield (a tough white cowboy), and I also competed twice at the big Pendleton Round Up in 1977 and 78, but I bucked off the horses both times. Charlie later won with another team at Pendleton in 1981. I bucked off so many horses and bulls that Charlie started calling me "Crash."

At the Fort Hall All-Indian Rodeo in August 1975, a bull named Avenger slammed me down pretty hard and broke my left arm. Hank Real Bird and another friend of ours, a bronc rider from the Warm Springs Reservation named Joe Scott, immediately ran over to help while I was sitting there in the arena holding my arm. Hank and Joe refused to let the local tribal emergency vehicle transport me to the hospital since the driver and his sidekick were both drunk. The tribal cops then arrested the two ambulance drivers and just left me sitting in the dirt there in the rodeo arena. Hank and Joe walked me over behind the bucking chutes and eventually a state cop hauled me to the hospital at Pocatello where I got an x-ray and a cast.

Years later whenever I ran into the rodeo announcer from that day at Fort Hall, Lonnie Racehorse, we always had a good time laughing about those two drunk Indian ambulance drivers and the tribal cops arresting them instead of giving me a ride to the hospital. Indian rodeo always provides lots of laughs.

A little while later during that summer of 1975, my friend Hank Real Bird broke his collar bone after bucking off a saddle bronc at a rodeo in Timber, Montana. We both were wearing slings on one arm so we each used our one good arm to haul furniture into an apartment we rented near Portland State University. We had to find a place to stay together since both of our girlfriends had kicked us out after our rodeo days ended that summer.

One time that fall Hank wanted to go eat at an inexpensive steakhouse in Portland. We'd had a few beers and forgot you needed two hands to cut steaks, so we had to take turns holding down our steaks with a fork while the other guy cut pieces with a knife. Hank and I used to laugh about that when we healed up later.

Hank was working at that time writing children's books and poetry for the NW Regional Education Lab in Portland, and I was at PSU School of Social Work. During that academic year of 1975-76 a couple of our friends, Jim St. Martin (Burns Paiute) and James Florendo (Warm Springs), would occasionally stay with us while in town. Both of them still like to tease me about the wall-to-wall Indians at a memorable party in that apartment.

During most of the 1970s I continued to play rugby full-time each spring and fall and ride in Indian rodeos and jackpot rodeos (small non-Indian rodeos not sanctioned by a regional pro rodeo association) in the summer. There were a couple weekends in the late spring where I played rugby on a Saturday and then rode in a rodeo on Sunday.

A long-time rugby teammate on both the Portland Pigs and Jesters rugby clubs was very interested in this rugby/rodeo combination. One day in 1975 he asked me to show him how to ride a bull. This guy, Jon Meads, is a NW rugby legend who is widely known by his nickname "The Troll." Troll is way smaller than the average rugby player, but he was totally fearless and probably pound-for-pound the toughest rugby player around. Since he's pretty short and stout, he always tackled opposing players very low to the ground so that even the biggest rugger carrying the ball was going down when Troll made contact. A rugby game wouldn't be complete until Troll had a bloody face from his fierce hits—which we teammates called his "face tackles."

In the spring of 1975 I took Troll to an indoor practice arena near Seaside, gave him a few pointers, loaned him my bull rope, and helped him down on his first bull. He then surprised everyone there by riding a fairly good bucking bull for the full 8 seconds. I couldn't believe it. None of us had ever seen a guy ride a bull successfully his very first time. He liked it so much that he continued riding bulls and playing rugby for a few years after that.

Since I decided after the 1977-78 rugby seasons that I needed to give up the continual wear and tear on my body from that sport, I decided to play more All-Indian basketball. In around 1976 I had met another Indian MSW named Larry Jordan from the Colville Tribe in Washington who was heavily involved with Indian basketball and All-Indian golf tournaments. Larry and his brothers, Mike and Tim, are real tall and were pretty well-known Indian basketball players in the NW. With Larry in Oregon and Washington, and later with others in Montana, I began playing in "Over 30" All-Indian Tournaments. Over 30 All-Indian Basketball is a lot like Old Boys Rugby—a bunch of older players who don't practice together and just get together for tournaments.

Indian basketball ("rez ball") is the perfect sport for Indian kids who grow up in poverty on the reservation, or in small reservation towns, since it doesn't require a lot of money to play. Just a hoop and a ball and you can play on most level surfaces, even hard packed dirt in the summer or winter. Basketball also fits in well on Indian reservations where our kids usually don't have the height or weight to play football—the money making sport. On Montana reservations, fast, skinny little Indian kids usually dominate in high school basketball. Rez ball actually serves as an outlet for the generational anger of whole tribal communities when they compete against white teams. It allows the warrior side of our usually introverted and gentle natures to be expressed.

Rez ball has been described as "controlled chaos, relentless pressure, constant trapping, and forcing your opponent into turnovers to get out and run. And run, run, run, run," Patrick Sauer in "The Legend of Elvis Old Bull", *Vice Sports* (October 30, 2014). Another article about rez ball describes its importance and dominance for tribal communities. "Though Indians constituted but 7% of Montana's population, their schools would win 10 Class A, B and C state high school basketball titles between 1980 and '90." Gary Smith, "Shadow of a Nation," *Sports Illustrated*, (February 18, 1991).

When I returned to Fort Belknap to work there in 1980 I played with some of my friends on our over 30 basketball team called "The Old Bulls." Our team chant, especially after the boys had a few beers, went like this: one of our players would shout, "What does the old bull say?" Someone else would shout, "Send more cows!" In 1984 we travelled to Larry Jordan's over 30 All-Indian basketball tournament on the Colville Reservation in Nespelem, Washington, and we took first place out of eight teams. I was the designated driver, since I was the only one sober, and I had to drive our van the whole 11 hours home to Fort Belknap while the boys drank more beer and kept shouting for more cows.

Recently a young Navajo lady in Portland didn't know what "teepee creeping" meant. That's because traditionally they live in "hogans" where she comes from down in New Mexico, so they don't use teepees as much. Another Montana guy and I then explained to her that teepee creeping is the Indian euphemism for sneaking around and "snagging", or "hooking up." With rugby, Indian rodeo, and Indian basketball during the 1970s, I must confess there was a lot of teepee creeping associated with each of these sports. Enough said.

While all this was going on, I decided to apply for a doctoral program at the University of Washington for the fall of 1976. My motivation at the time was simply to seek legitimacy to teach at the university level. It seemed that at PSU I wasn't quite regarded as a legitimate university instructor with only a Master of Social Work (MSW) degree. So, with the recommendation of Dr. Gordon Hearn, Dean of the PSU School Social of Work, and a psychology professor at PSU (whose name escapes me), plus doing ok on the GRE (Graduate Record Examinations), I was accepted at the UW Graduate School of Education.

During the 1976-80 academic years I managed to complete all the course work, dissertation defense, and the survey research data needed for a doctoral dissertation at the UW. In the dissertation study I researched two learning variables called

Locus of Control and Field Dependence/Independence among Indian undergraduate and graduate students. In my study it turned out that both locus of control and field independence/ dependence were related to perceived success for both Indian undergrad and grad students.

I couldn't have completed those four years of my doctoral program without the help of Dr. Robert Ryan (Lakota), Director of the *White Cloud Center* at the Oregon Health Sciences University in Portland. While I was in school at the UW, Dr. Ryan hired me on a very flexible half-time work schedule to provide training and technical assistance for some of his tribal mental health research contracts. Dr. Ryan and his staff also provided great emotional and technical support while I struggled through some difficult research courses at the UW.

After completing all the course work and gathering dissertation data in the spring, I decided to go home to work at the Fort Belknap Indian Reservation in August 1980. My life of rugby and rodeo were over and I was having a hard time quitting drinking. It might have been another crazy decision, but it just seemed like the right time to go home.

All-Indian Rodeo at Portland, Oregon (1978)
CL Scott photo collection

All-Indian Rodeo at Tygh Valley, Oregon (1979)
CL Scott photo collection

Chapter 11
Going Home, Getting Sober, and Triathlon

In the spring of 1978 I had decided to retire from rugby after playing every year since 1966. What was left after 12 years of full-time rugby? I was really depressed. I didn't realize how dependent I'd become on the physicality and comradery of the game, and the socially acceptable excuse it gave me for heavy drinking. Without rugby I was emotionally lost, but I never told anyone at the time. I still had two more years of doctoral studies in Seattle to get through, and I still had Indian rodeo and Indian basketball, but I was living with a great deal of depression and loneliness without rugby.

This might sound strange, but to me Indian rodeo wasn't as tough on my body as rugby. Riding a bucking horse or a bull in a rodeo only lasts for eight seconds and then it's all over. You're either hurt or not, and then it's time to go off drinking with the boys and try to snag those cowgirls. With rugby it's the twice weekly sprints and physical contact in practices and then games on Saturdays, or playing in weekend tournaments. This lasts for several weeks at a time each spring and fall. After 12 years it took a heavy physical toll on my body. So, it was finally time in the spring of 1978 to hang up my rugby cleats after the Monterey National Rugby Tournament that year.

My drinking wasn't fun anymore without rugby those last two years in Seattle at the UW from 1978 to 1980. I finally had to admit to myself that I was too dependent on drinking for most social interactions with others. Without telling anyone, I began trying to not drink at all, or only occasionally have a few beers. It didn't work. This was especially clear when I played in four All-Indian Over 30 basketball tournaments at Yakima, Nisqually, and Nespelem in Washington state, and at the Chemawa Indian School in Salem, Oregon. Not drinking with the boys after games was miserable, and I always failed to stay sober.

It felt like 1980 was the tipping point. I'd finished my doctoral course work in Seattle with only the dissertation left to write. I was really depressed without rugby, and I was unable to stop drinking on my own. As one crazy solution, I decided that summer to go home and work for my tribe in Montana—a typical "geographic cure" that so many alcoholics try unsuccessfully. How crazy is that, believing that going home to a heavy drinking environment would make me feel better?

At an NIEA (National Indian Education Association) conference in the late 1970s, one of the keynote speakers talked about going home to work at her reservation after finishing college. This Indian lady said in order to go home to work for your own tribe, "you have to be either brilliant or crazy." When I went home to work at Fort Belknap in 1980 I was probably closer to the crazy side.

So, in August 1980 I was hired and began work as the tribal health planner at Fort Belknap. The next year we were awarded a small Montana state-funded grant to start a group home for kids on our reservation, and I went to work there as the director. George Shields, a respected Assiniboine elder, named our program the Wild Horse Youth Ranch, and he worked with us as a Foster Grandparent. He said that Wild Horse Butte, which is just a few miles south of the agency, had good spirits and that would help our kids. The group home could house 10 tribal youths—five boys on one side and five girls on the other.

The Wild Horse Youth Ranch was created as a residential group home for tribal kids needing a safe place to stay while awaiting family reunification, or a suitable tribal foster home placement. A great effort was made by our staff and friends and relatives to provide a positive and culturally-based, healthy environment for the kids

Most of my last two years of drinking while working at Fort Belknap during 1980-82 were really miserable. Then on Labor Day Weekend in 1982 I drove to Cannon Beach, Oregon for our Annual Lifeguards Reunion and finally had my last drink. I'd thrown up again (like usual), blacked out (like usual), and didn't remember how I got back to my friend Dick Rankin's house that night (like usual). The next day I left the beach with a huge hangover and was really depressed while driving back to Montana. During that long 900 mile drive home I made the decision to give up the booze for good.

When I got home to Fort Belknap I decided to attend a little AA meeting on the reservation that was being held on Thursday nights in a trailer behind the old government hospital where my two sisters and I were born. Some of my relatives and non-drinking friends had started that meeting a while back and attendance rarely exceeded a dozen tribal members. On Thursday night, September 5, 1982, I told my friends and relatives at the meeting, "my name is John, and I'm an alcoholic." The group busted out laughing—they all knew how I drank. You can't hide much on a small reservation like Fort Belknap.

With the acceptance and support of that little group, I jumped full tilt boogie into sobriety. Our little group of sober Fort Belknap Indians had a lot of fun travelling together to AA meetings held weekly in the small reservation border towns of Chinook, Harlem, and Havre. We also drove to AA roundups held in Billings, Butte, and Kalispell. My decision to quit drinking was a huge emotional relief, and I owe at lot to those great folks in the Fort Belknap AA group.

During the first five years of my sobriety (1982-87) we also participated in annual Intertribal Sobriety Campouts that began in 1983 at the Northern Cheyenne Reservation. At this first Campout I ran into my old rodeo buddy, Hank Real Bird, and he invited me to a sweat lodge ceremony alongside the Little Bighorn River on the Crow Reservation with his brothers, Richard and Kennard. After the sweat we jumped into the river to cool off and had a good visit. This was a real nice memory with some good old Indian rodeo cowboys.

The Campout rotated each summer to one of the seven reservations in Montana and we had our first Sobriety Campout at Fort Belknap in 1984 in the little Rocky Mountains at Mission Canyon. We were really surprised when our head cook, Honey Doney, reported that 1,200 people showed up for the Saturday evening dinner at the campout.

Quite a few Canadians used to come down to attend our Sobriety Campouts in Montana. Once at a campout on the Fort Peck Reservation, two First Nation ladies were there and one whispered to me, "What's a DWI? I keep hearing people talk about getting a DWI." I replied that it meant "Drinking with Indians" and she punched me hard on the shoulder.

In Montana a DWI actually meant Driving While Intoxicated, but we Indians like to twist the English language around just for fun, often in small, self-deprecating ways. At Fort Belknap, for example, one of my Assiniboine friends asked me, "Hey John, what do you call two Gros Ventres in a sweat lodge?" Answer: "Gorillas in the Mist." Another sober friend at Fort Belknap told me that my PhD actually meant "poor helpless drunk."

Use of humor in almost any situation is a huge part of our survival and resilience for healing in Indian Country. Pow wow MCs always crack the most corny jokes imaginable and love to tease everyone. Even traditional Indian elders often surprise guests and researchers with some hard teasing and real earthy talk.

I ended up working seven years at Fort Belknap and I have mostly good memories from that time, but quitting drinking was the main takeaway for me from the decade of the 1980s. My first five years of sobriety were spent at Fort Belknap, and I often say at Indian AA meetings around Portland and Seattle that if I could stay sober on my reservation I could stay sober anywhere. The only negative experiences or regrets from those years at home were related to drinking, otherwise I have great memories while working with my tribe.

During those seven years at home in 1980-87 I worked as the tribal health planner, group home director, parenting project coordinator, tribal councilman, and tribal college president. After I sobered up in 1982, I also became a foster parent for three of our tribal kids who lived at the youth ranch. Tony, Charlie Brown, and Ellie were three great kids who also became positive mentors for the other group home kids. We used to hit all the pow wows in Montana and had a great time together.

Being elected to serve on one's tribal council is an honor for any tribal member and I was grateful to be selected to represent the Gros Ventre Tribe during 1983-86. The stress and time commitment while on council can be challenging, but I was fortunate to serve with some good folks and have many fond memories from that time. Tribal council members I served with were Charlie Bear, Leo Brockie, Prince Brockie, Davey Hawley, Harvey King, Chappie Long Fox, Snuffy Main, Warren Matte, Randy Perez, Bill Snell, Chub Snell, and Lyman Young. Any differences of opinions we had were eventually smoothed over with respect and lots of Indian humor. From what I've seen or heard about others' experiences serving on their tribal councils, it looks like I was pretty lucky.

At Fort Belknap you can't be on the council and work for the tribe at the same time, so I had to resign from the council in 1986 in order to work as president of Fort Belknap Tribal College—now called Aaniiih Nakoda College (ANC). We had been told that to obtain accreditation by the accrediting body based in Seattle, a tribal college was strongly recommended to have a doctoral level president. I was scheduled to have my dissertation defense in December 1986, so I fit the bill. My first academic year at the tribal college was enjoyable for the teaching and student interactions and we were successful in obtaining college accreditation, but I didn't really like all the paperwork and mundane details of tribal college administration. So after a little over one year it was time to try something else.

In November 1987 I decided to leave Fort Belknap to begin work as director of the Thunderbird Treatment Center in Seattle. Besides wanting to return to work in the substance abuse field. I'd been seeing a lady at Fort Belknap who was incapable of maintaining a healthy relationship. Out of respect for her privacy and anonymity I won't say anymore about that here. It was just another powerful motive to seek a geographic cure, and suffice it to say, it worked out for the better.

In Seattle I worked for six months during the winter of 1987-88 at Thunderbird Treatment Center, and we passed the Commission on Accreditation of Rehabilitation Facilities (CARF) during that time. I then worked another six months in 1988 for the Indian Health Service Office in Seattle as an adolescent substance abuse counselor. In this latter position I worked half-time with kids at the Puyallup Tribe and half-time on the Muckleshoot Reservation. Then in December 1988 I left

Seattle to work with the student substance abuse program at Chemawa Indian School in Salem, Oregon.

I had decided to give up rugby in 1978 and in 1987, at age 46, I rode my last bull in a rodeo at Chinook, Montana, but I still needed some type of physical challenge with a lower risk than rugby and rodeo, so the sport of triathlon became the answer for the next 21 years (1987-2008).

Triathlon combines swimming, biking, and running, although one race in Montana substituted canoe racing down a river for the swimming event. Training and competing in these events helped keep me sober and motivated to seek good health. In 1987, beginning at Bozeman, Montana, I've completed over 70 events in California, Idaho, Montana, Utah, and Washington. There were four times when I didn't finish the course. This was due to a sunken canoe one time and a flat bike tire another time in Montana, getting in the wrong lane at an indoor pool in Oregon, and getting froze out in the mountains before the run portion at a race near Lake Tahoe. I managed to complete three ironman distance events, however. Two were in Northern California in 1990 and 91, and one in Utah in 2002. An ironman triathlon consists of a 2.4 mile swim, 112 mile bike, and 26.2 mile run.

After developing asthma in 2002, I had to cut way back on the longer endurance events and only compete in the shorter sprint-distance triathlons. A sprint triathlon includes various distances up to a half-mile in the swim, a 12 mile bike, and 3.1 mile run. My last sprint triathlon was at Blue Lake in Portland in 2008. I won my age group, but it was time to quit while I was ahead.

Erik and me at a Whitman College Lacrosse match in Seattle (1988)
John Spence photo collection

Vineman Ironman Triathlon at Santa Rosa, California (1991)
John Spence photo collection

Chapter 12
Chemawa, Grand Ronde, and BJ

In the fall of 1988 I was working in Seattle when three friends who worked at Chemawa Indian School in Salem, Oregon began recruiting me to take the director position of a student substance abuse program on campus called the Chemawa Alcohol Education Center (CAEC). I'd known these friends for several years (Jake and Lori Bighorn, and Patrick Melendey) and the program sounded interesting. After meeting the CAEC counseling staff on campus and speaking with a few of the students, I agreed to take the job and started work there in December 1988.

With the history of abuses and cultural loss faced by thousands of Indian kids at boarding schools, and my grandmother's traumatic experience at the Catholic mission boarding school on our reservation, it's ironic that I'd end up at Chemawa. Even more surprising was discovering after I'd gone to work there that both my mother and birth father had attended Chemawa. I don't know why our grandmother never told me this, and I don't know the details of her childhood boarding school experience, but it must have contributed to that part of our typical dysfunctional family ethic of "don't talk, don't trust, don't feel."

Founded in 1880, Chemawa is the oldest existing federal Indian boarding school in the USA. The school no longer tolerates physical abuse by staff or teachers, and over the years it has evolved into an alternative high school for at-risk Indian kids. At the CAEC program we served about 200 students each school year who were referred to us for substance abuse incidents. The CAEC staff involved students with individual assessments and crisis interventions, weekly counseling groups, sweat lodges, off-campus recreation therapy, and adventure-based activities on the weekends.

During my last two years at Chemawa I was asked to coach the track and cross country teams. One of our kids won at the state cross country meet, but the highlight for the kids was when Billy Mills (Lakota) attended a large invitational meet at Chemawa in 1994. Billy is the only American to win the Gold Medal in the 10,000 meter run at the Olympics. His victory at the 1964 Olympics in Tokyo is considered the greatest upset in Olympic history. Billy was really gracious and attentive with every one of our students who wanted to meet him.

During seven years working there (1988-95) the number of alcohol or drug write-ups went down each year. As CAEC director I supervised an all-Indian staff of five or six counselors (Heather Crow, Jamie Fraser, Thomas Ghost Dog, Calvin Hecocta, Clayton Schutz, Pat Web) and a receptionist (Grace Chandler). We also had two full-time recreation therapists (Ed Barlett and David Graham) assigned to the program from the Indian Health Service who attended our weekly staff meetings and organized weekly off-campus activities. We had a pretty good student substance abuse program going for those seven years until the School Board made an ill-informed decision in 1995 that pretty much killed the program.

In the spring of 1995 the Bureau of Indian Affairs Superintendent at Chemawa manipulated the School Board into voting to allow him to supervise our program at CAEC. At that point I resigned rather than work under this tyrannical BIA federal bureaucrat. The School Board later learned this move was illegal since my staff and I were employed through an Indian Health Service contract. The School Superintendent was a BIA federal official who couldn't legally supervise another federally-funded Indian Health Service contract program like CAEC. The School Board President then called me to ask if I would return to Chemawa, but I had already committed to work for the Confederated Tribes of Grand Ronde at their adolescent treatment center in Keizer, Oregon.

After one year at the tribal youth treatment center, I directed the tribal social services department for two more years at Grand Ronde. After three years at Grand Ronde I left in 1998 to begin independent contract work with the nine Oregon Tribes and a few Indian non-profits. I still have lots of good friends at Grand Ronde and often attend their pow wow, the Canoe Journey, and the Agency Creek Round Dance.

While working at Chemawa I met BJ (Betty Jean) Repp. BJ had worked at CAEC during the 1987-88 school year to complete a practicum experience required for her Human Services degree at Chemeketa Community College. We were introduced to each other during the summer of 1990 and two years later she asked me to teach a class at Chemeketa. That led to our first date in 1992 and we were destined to be together for the next 22 years.

BJ helped me set up a small business in tribal consulting when I left Grand Ronde in 1998 and this has worked out well with over 70 contracts since then. One long-term contract was teaching part-time for 20 years in the School of Social Work at Portland State University. Another long-term contract has been with the Native American Rehabilitation Association/NW (NARA), the comprehensive prevention, treatment, and wellness center in Portland founded in 1970.

I especially like the flexibility in the Scope of Work for my main current contract at NARA that reads: "program development, grant writing, horses, and other duties as assigned." Another main series of contracts has been with the Native Wellness Institute (NWI) based in Gresham, Oregon. NWI was founded in 2000 and is involved with lots of tribal community organizing and healing work in Indian Country. A fellow tribal member, Jillene Joseph (A'aninin) is the founder and director. She and her team have done great prevention and healing work all over Indian Country, as well as with Indigenous peoples in Hawaii, Australia, and New Zealand.

When we started seeing each other in 1992 BJ was just beginning work toward a Masters degree in the College Student Services program at Oregon State University. She was successful in completing that degree and then went straight into a doctoral program at OSU. After her daughter Joy graduated from high school in 1994, the three of us moved into a small house in Salem. A year later BJ and I were married in August 1995.

Many things contributed to our good times together during those 22 years. When we met BJ was sober for five years and I had 10 years of sobriety. Our kids, her daughter Joy and my son Erik, got along well. BJ was an extrovert and I'm an introvert, but that actually complemented our relationship. Our politics were far to the left, and we both made each other laugh a lot. Our disagreements could be heavy at times, but we respected each other's positions and any differences were resolved eventually. A couple of times that required marriage counseling—but hey, more couples should try that.

BJ was a good athlete and we completed several individual and team triathlons together. On our honeymoon in the San Juan Islands in Puget Sound we rented kayaks and rowed next to some sea otters. This was a beautiful experience, so as soon as we got home to Salem we bought two kayaks that we used a lot over the years. We surfed and snow skied together, rode horses together, ran a marathon and half-marathon together, and went on lots of hikes.

BJ was an up-the-down-staircase-person, a fearless risk-taker who enjoyed pushing the envelope in her work while tirelessly advocating for adult and non-traditional college students. While she was Director of Extended Studies at PSU she helped hundreds of students successfully complete their bachelor degrees. She always cheered for the underdog and was a fierce social justice warrior. Folks in the Marion County Democratic Central Committee could always count on her for help with protests against the Iraq War and canvassing for progressive political candidates.

BJ loved animals and we wound up with eight cats at different times during our 22 years together. She actually stole one of these cats from a neighbor when we were moving from the first little house we shared with Joy in 1995 to a larger one in 2001. BJ was convinced that our somewhat shady neighbors weren't taking good care of their two large dogs and their scrawny little cat so she just took that cat with us the day we moved, even though we already had four other cats at the time (Persephone, Rusty, Toughie, and Blackie). Stealing a cat that she felt was neglected or abused—that was so BJ. That skinny little cat, Junior, ended up outliving all the rest of our other cats.

While she was going to school at Chemeketa and Joy was attending South Salem High School, they survived in near poverty as a single mother and daughter. She told me a very moving story one time. She and Joy had to share a burger and fries because they were too poor to afford a complete meal together before she received her next scholarship check. That story really touched me, and now whenever I drive by the Burger Basket in Salem it's hard to keep back the tears.

To BJ and Joy, family was everything. BJ was always the one to organize family dinners with her parents. She usually had to push her two brothers and two sisters to be there and to include their kids. Without BJ organizing and pushing her siblings, most of her family gatherings probably wouldn't have happened. Joy has inherited that gracious trait and wondrous energy from her mother. Joy's house is now the center for family dinners and holiday gatherings.

When Joy was 17 years old, BJ and my sister Marsha decided that our families needed to revive Marsha's earlier tradition of spending a few days each summer at Cannon Beach, Oregon with the kids. When all our kids were little, Marsha used to take her three kids (Steve, Nicole, and Stacee) to the beach, and I would bring my son Erik. When the kids grew older, however, it became difficult to get them together in the summer. With BJ and Marsha scheming together, they made this happen again. Because of BJ and Marsha, our annual family gatherings have continued for over 20 years at Cannon Beach.

During Christmas 2013, BJ and I visited her brother David and his husband Bill in Los Angeles, and later we joined her sister Karolin and husband Pete in San Diego. On our drive back to Salem on New Year's Day 2014, BJ began to experience stomach pains. When we got home the pains became more frequent, and eventually bad enough for us to drive to the emergency room at Providence Hospital in southwest Portland.

More hospital visits and tests followed most of that month of January. Finally, a family meeting was scheduled with Joy and her husband David, BJ's sister Karolin, and I to meet with an oncologist on January 23, 2014 to learn the diagnosis and recommended treatment. The doctor told us it was pancreatic cancer, but didn't really tell us in detail what that meant. In her typical forthright manner BJ ordered the doctor to tell us if it was terminal, and if so, how much time did she have left. The doctor replied that it might only be four to six months.

We were devastated, but we held out hope that because of BJ's excellent physical health and positive attitude we could extend that time, or even beat this thing. Despite everyone's best efforts, however, she took the journey four months later on May 7, 2014.

I don't want to recount everything that we tried or how painful and difficult this was for BJ and all of us. That's a story that many other families are painfully familiar with, and I don't want to dwell on this here. We all just want to remember the BJ we knew—the wonder woman, teacher, counselor, social justice warrior. The best wife, mother, grandmother, sister, and friend that one could be fortunate to know.

Joy wrote this statement about her mother that we submitted as part of the *BJ Repp, PhD, Memorial Scholarship* that we established at Chemeketa Community College:

> My mom was the best! Remembering her illness and our battle is very emotional. I remember her strength. I remember her kindness, her generosity and her larger than life personality. She had a very silly sense of humor and a zest for life. She was exuberant!
>
> She saw her role as the Director of Extended Studies at PSU as a mission to help educate and change lives for the better, everywhere, and for everyone. ESPECIALLY those with challenges, disadvantages and hardships. As a community member, she was continually contributing to her environment. She helped establish and open the first Multicultural Center in my home town. She was always involved in local politics helping to shape our

local environment to include marginalized groups and being a champion for a warm and accepting community.

In life my mom knew no boundaries. She adventured and traveled. She was happy, spunky, silly, funny and fun. When mom would visit my home, she would walk in, and immediately drop everything in her arms and chase my babies around, grab them, hug them, kiss them, and squeeze them as they squealed with delight. I believe if it were socially acceptable, that is how she would have entered all rooms. She loved to play, have fun and make people feel special.

When she was diagnosed with stage IV cancer she begged the doctors for a "30 year plan" so she could watch my kids grow up. When we realized that was not possible she would vent to my husband. Spittin' mad, she would swear and yell, she didn't want to go before she could watch my kiddos grow up. My husband was just the right audience for her anger. He could relate to her and cussed and got mad right along with her. But in my presence and around the kids, she was calm and loving and patient. She hid her fear, hurt, and anger from us so we could all enjoy our short time together. My stepfather, John Spence, was the love of her life and he took care of her with love and nurturing. We both spent many nights with mom through her illness. The nights were the hardest. And, as we watched her health deteriorate, we leaned on each other more and more. We were all heart broken at her passing, but John knew he wanted to continue her life long mission of helping others, we he started a scholarship fund in her name and here we are. Both John and I want people to know how much she touched the world around her and keep helping as she would have done.

Oh, we used to laugh, she was so funny. She was witty and just a little mischievous. We would laugh until it hurt and our eyes were crying. She was a great mom. She was a great friend. She was straight and honest and she loved with her whole heart. I love you mom and I miss you today, almost 5 years gone now. We will keep remembering and telling others of your love, exuberance and generosity.

BJ seemed to know the words to every old song on the radio and she was a really great dancer. A song by Jackson Browne tells the exact words for how I felt about BJ near the end—"For a Dancer."

> *I don't remember losing track of you*
> *You were always dancing in and out of view*
> *I must have thought you'd always be around*

BJ and Ruby at Cannon Beach (2010)
Joy C. Lincke photo collection

BJ and me in Salem (2002)
BJ Repp photo collection

BJ and me in Salem (2002)
BJ Repp photo collection

BJ, Joy, and Ruby (2010)
BJ Repp photo collection

Erik at Cannon Beach (2010)
BJ Repp photo collection

Chapter 13
Standing Rock and other Battles

On September 3, 2016, mercenaries hired by the Dakota Access Pipeline (DAPL) set attack dogs on tribal people who were trying to protect sacred sites at the Standing Rock Sioux Reservation in North Dakota. Amy Goodwin of *Democracy Now!* Was there at the time and filmed a seven-minute video of that dog attack. A friend, Dr. Danica Love Brown, was shown in the video trying to keep the mercenaries and their dogs from attacking our people. The video immediately went viral, rallying tribal people all over Indian Country to go to Standing Rock to help stop the pipeline.

Two days later, on September 5 (my 35th sobriety birthday) I started driving the 1,300 miles by myself on my first trip from Beaverton, Oregon to Standing Rock. The main camp there, Oceti Sakowin (Seven Council Fires), was made up of many smaller camps that were centered around the sacred fire started by elders of the Standing Rock Sioux Tribe. When I arrived on September 7 I didn't know where exactly to go, but figured I could find friends from Oregon who I knew had arrived there earlier. As soon as I drove into camp I ran into Sam "Huey" Nelson (Lakota) who I'd known for several years in Portland. Sam told me to go to the Nelson/Archambault camp where his dad, John "Buzz" Nelson was also staying. After I found him, Buzz introduced me to others at that camp and everyone was very welcoming.

My sister, Avis Archambault, flew up from Arizona that same day, on September 7, and I picked her up at the airport in Bismarck, North Dakota. We barely made it back to camp through the barricades set up by the Morton County cops and the National Guard. We both then stayed at the Nelson/Archambault camp for several days.

Our camp included the world-famous "Winona's Kitchen." Winona Kasto (Lakota) ruled that part of the camp as a highly regarded and well-known "traditional cook." Her meal times became large, happy gatherings where no one was turned away. She would even have one of her relatives stand out front of the kitchen at meal times and invite anyone walking by to come in and eat.

Our long-deceased grandfather, Sam Archambault, was from Standing Rock, but Avis and Marsha and I were raised at Fort Belknap, Montana so we didn't know many of our relatives in North Dakota. Avis and I soon began meeting all kinds of our Archambault cousins that we didn't know and this was very special for us. The Tribal Chairman, David Archambault II, and his dad David, Sr., were very welcoming and took good care of Avis after I had to leave a few days later to return to work in Oregon.

A few weeks prior to our arrival, David II had been arrested while protesting construction of the pipeline on traditional tribal land. This despicable action by a corporate- empowered police force had already caused thousands of Indian and non-Indian allies to come to camp before the dog attacks. In an editorial in *The New York Times* shortly after his arrest, Chairman Archambault explained what happened this way:

> Perhaps only in North Dakota, where oil tycoons wine and dine elected officials, and where the governor, Jack Dalrymple, serves as an advisor to the Trump

campaign, would state and county governments act as the armed enforcement for corporate interests.

After the *Democracy Now!* Video, Avis and I just had to go to the camp. Like so many others we were horrified by the dog attacks on our people, and because of the video the camp swelled by thousands more people from across Indian Country and all over the globe. The *New York Times* estimated that over 14,000 people were there later in December when about 3,000 veterans arrived to protect the camp.

The day after Avis and I arrived, we joined thousands of others on a long march led by elders up to the spot north of camp where our people were attacked by the dogs on September 3. No cops showed up there to prevent tribal elders from bringing out their pipes and conducting a healing ceremony. While at the ceremony, Avis and I were surprised to run into a couple of our relatives who had just driven 510 miles from Fort Belknap. Our cousins, Ruben Horseman and Marlene Stiffarm, then invited us to join them after the ceremony for a dinner of caribou soup at their camp.

The next day everyone at the camp was surprised and happy when the US Army Corps of Engineers denied DAPL's permit for continuing construction of the pipeline. A couple of days later I had to return to work on a contract for grant writing with NARA/NW and another contract for teaching at Portland State University. Avis was able to stay a few days longer at camp and had a great time visiting with our many Archambault relatives there.

Despite denial of the pipeline permit by the Corps of Engineers in September, DAPL just went ahead with construction of the "black snake" while legal challenges dragged on in the federal courts. A militarized force of county and state cops and National Guard troops grew much larger, they surrounded the camp, and their violence escalated toward the "water protectors" during October and November.

Young men and women in the Red Warrior Camp and others at the larger Oceti Sakowin camp were enraged at this and took several direct actions on the front lines to stop construction of the pipeline. In October, county and state cops and federal troops launched several brutal attacks on the water protectors with beatings, tear gas, mace, compression grenades, and painful rubber bullets. In November, they shot ice cold water cannons on the people during freezing weather. Hundreds of arrests followed, and many water protectors were detained in overcrowded cages with little heat and food and were denied speedy legal representation. The great majority of charges against these folks were later dropped.

President Obama and the courts did nothing to stop these vicious attacks on our people, even though in November a United Nations Special Rapporteur on human rights issued a statement decrying these brutal attacks. Mr. Maina Kai said 400 people held during the demonstrations had suffered "inhuman and degrading conditions in detention," (*UN News*, 15 November 2016). This betrayal by Obama and our federal "trustees" at the Bureau of Indian Affairs and the Indian Health Service reinforced for many of us what we had always known—US government agencies and most of our elected officials really don't give a damn about the Native people of this land.

Under the guise of stopping the violence to protect white citizens in the surrounding communities, the governor of North Dakota ordered the Oceti Sakowin camp to be cleared out on December 5, 2016. In response to the governor's order and to protect the camp from more violence and eviction, an estimated 3,000 Veterans and supporters began arriving at camp in early December.

At that time I made my second trip there by joining a caravan of nine vehicles of veterans who left Portland on December 2 for Standing Rock to protect the camp. After arriving early in the morning on December 4, another Marine from Fort Belknap (Andrew Gray) and I were invited to sleep in the Sitting Bull teepee set up by the Archambault family. A couple of days later I was invited to sleep in a small heated shed occupied by Char Bad Cobb (Lakota) and Sam Nelson. Most of our other veterans from the Portland caravan stayed in one of the large military tents set up by Standing Rock supporters.

On December 5 no cops or National Guard troops showed up to close down the camp as the North Dakota governor had ordered. The previous day on December 4, the US Army Corps of Engineers denied DAPL's permit to continue construction of the pipeline until an environmental impact assessment (EIS) was completed. A powerful blizzard set in later the night of December 5 and the next day the tribal casino invited veterans to camp inside to get relief from the severe cold. Hundreds of us slept on the auditorium floor in the casino and food service staff opened up their buffet for us.

During the blizzard many people were stranded by the heavy snow and lack of visibility prevented travel. At the Nelson/ Archambault camp, Char Bad Cobb and John Sanchez (Carizo/ Shoshone-Bannock) jumped into John's chained up 4-wheel drive truck to rescue people who were stranded along the road. Char and John saved several people from freezing to death. There were hundreds of acts of courage and kindness like that at the camp.

After the pipeline permit was denied on December 4 and a victory celebration was held, tribal elders asked visitors to leave camp and the Standing Rock Sioux Tribe would continue with the court process. Our group of veterans then began traveling home on December 7. On the way back we dropped off Andrew

Gray in Billings and we all made it safely back to Portland after a long drive over icy and snowy roads.

Most of us suspected that because of the November 2016 presidential election, denial of the pipeline permit by the Corps of Engineers would not be honored. Sure enough, our suspicions were correct when in February 2017 one of the first actions Trump took was to overturn the Corps' order—without even waiting for an environmental impact assessment. Anger grew at this continuing betrayal by the federal government and many folks refused to leave Oceti Sakowin. According to some of our friends who had taken more supplies to camp from Portland in January, the previous happy atmosphere and good morale in the camp began to deteriorate, and eventually the government forced out all campers on February 22, 2017.

Some of us who had been at Oceti Sakowin, or had raised money for the camp through several rallies in the Portland area, decided to keep the fire going that had started at Standing Rock. John Sanchez and Linda Looking (Lakota) were our main fund raisers and organizers and wanted to keep the fight going for clean water and Indigenous rights. Buzz Nelson (Lakota) presided as our elder and spiritual leader when we started the Pacific Northwest Council of Water Protectors (PNWCP) in February 2017.

John Sanchez then left for Florida in February at the invitation of some folks in the Miccosukee Tribe whom he had met at Standing Rock. The tribal folks in Florida asked his help in setting up a spirit camp on their tribal land in the Everglades to fight against two environmental threats to their homelands. These two issues were the proposed "River of Grass Greenway" (ROGG) that would run 76 miles between Naples and Miami and a proposal to begin fracking for oil in the Everglades.

At John's request, seven of us in the PNWCP drove to Florida in March to join him in helping the tribe set up their sacred fire and spirit camp in the Everglades a few miles east of Naples. Camping in the Everglades was a little scary for us when we learned about alligators traveling at night between the nearby ponds where we set up camp. We were also warned about snakes, bears, and panthers that were often seen in that area. While we were camped there, a bear twice tried to break into our food storage shed, and we always saw alligators in the ponds close to our camp. Linda Looking started calling one of the alligators "Boots." Mosquitoes in the Everglades were maddening, but they didn't seem to bother the local Miccosukee tribal members as much.

While at the camp in March we joined the tribe and many environmental supporters on a protest march against the River of Grass Greenway that began along the highway from tribal headquarters east toward Miami. Some of us had to return to work in Oregon so we were only able to join the march for a few miles. Later we were elated to learn that the Miami-Dade County Board of Commissioners ruled against construction of the ROGG.

The next month during April my friend Art McConville (Cayuse/Nez Perce), a Marine Corps combat veteran in Vietnam, and I decided to return to the spirit camp in the Everglades for an Earth Day celebration organized by the Miccosukee Tribe and several non-Indian environmental allies. We drove the 3,200 miles from Beaverton, Oregon to Naples, Florida in only 40 hours in my old Chevy one-ton pickup (affectionately called "The Beast"). Folks at the spirit camp were looking for a truck to haul donated supplies, so Art and I decided to drive my old pickup down there to donate it to the camp.

How crazy is that—two old Indian guys in their 70s driving cross country in an old Chevy truck with over 300,000 miles on it? Our friends in the Pacific NW Council of Water Protectors thought we were crazy, but we're both Marines and every Jarhead is a little crazy anyway—and we like it that way. We were only stopped once by a cop in Georgia who didn't quite buy our story, but he finally just laughed it off and let us go. I guess Art and I don't look that dangerous any more.

The PNW Council of Water Protectors has continued to meet and organize against environmental threats in our area. The Council has supported the fight against expansion of the Zenith Energy gas terminal in Portland and construction of the liquefied natural gas (LNG) pipeline and Jordan Cove export terminal in Coos Bay, Oregon. LNG would destroy tribal sacred sites in Oregon and could damage over 500 separate waterways. The pipeline would terminate at a shipping point to Asia in Jordan Cove. Dredging in Jordan Cove would destroy an environmentally sensitive shellfish and fishing area.

In February 2020 the Oregon State Department of Land Conservation and Development voted to deny the LNG pipeline and the Jordan Cove terminal. Then the Federal Environmental Regulation Commission (FERC), on a 2-1 vote approved LNG and Jordan Cove in March 2020. On January19, 2021, however, as reported by *The Oregonian*, FERC reversed their position and backed the state's denial of the permitting process for LNG and Jordan Cove. Tribal and environmental groups won this battle.

Several of us in the PNW Council of Water Protectors continue to participate in strategies and rallies against other threats to clean water and tribal sovereignty. Linda Looking and her daughters are often invited to sing traditional Lakota healing songs at large environmental or human rights gatherings in this area and Art McConnville is often asked to start off water ceremonies.

Our friends Rowena Jackson (Klamath) and Toma Deavers (Cherokee) have been especially active in the fight against LNG and Jordan Cove and the proposed telescope construction on

Mauna Kea in Hawaii. At the Klamath Tribes, Ka'ila Farrell-Smith, Taylor Tupper, and Chairman Don Gentry were very active in opposing LNG and Jordan Cove. Rowena and Toma have also organized solidarity rallies to support the Wet'suwet'en people in Canada against construction of a pipeline on their lands.

Since 2018 the Council has also organized an annual Medicine Gathering at Oxbow Park on the Sandy River just a little ways east of Portland. It has become a perfect occasion for Indigenous folks and non-Indian allies in our area to gather and share information about protecting our water and earth mother. Linda Looking (we call her "the Boss") has been called "the heart and soul" of the Gathering. She has been successful in organizing the participation of several traditional tribal people, as well as local non-profits and environmental agencies. Another Council member, Nico Wind Cordova (Assiniboine/Ojibwa/Lakota), an immensely talented singer and band leader, has helped with fundraising for the Gathering through several donated performances. Ted Drier, Kay Eagle Staff, Charmaine Kinney, John Sanchez, Cedar Sanders, Christopher Trochie, and D'ana Valenzuela have all contributed lots of time and energy to make the Gatherings happen. Jillene Joseph of the Native Wellness Institute (NWI) has helped us gather and prepare food and Jillene's team at NWI provides Native games for the younger camp participants.

Many of us in the PNW Council of Water Protectors have also been involved in supporting the Black Lives Matter (BLM) protests that have been held for over 100 days during the summer and fall of 2020 in Portland. Indigenous community members here participate in a weekly sunrise ceremony to support BLM and the continuing fight for social justice. Lately the ceremony has taken place at the Red House, a property owned by a mixed Black and Indigenous family that is unfairly being evicted due to predatory lending practices and a long-time gentrification process in a historic Black neighborhood in north Portland.

At Standing Rock and other battles, I'm grateful for the support of my family, relatives, and many AA buddies. All this has allowed my small part in the greater movement for recovery and healing in Indian Country.

Sign at the camp (2016)
Nico Wind Cordova photo collection

Avis and me at Standing Rock (2016)
Avis Archambault photo collection

Art McConville and Veterans at Standing Rock (2016)
Cheryl Lucas photo collection

Andrew Gray and me with Standing Rock Veterans (2016)
Chery Lucas photo collection

Buzz and Sam Nelson, me, Billy Wilson (2017)
Christopher Trotchie photo collection

PNW Council of Water Protectors (2017)
Nico Wind Cordova photo collection

Chapter 14
Recovery and Healing in Indian Country

Who knows what would have happened to my two sisters and me if it wasn't for our grandmother, Molly Cochran Archambault, and our uncle Bryan Archambault? Before the Indian Child Welfare Act (ICWA) of 1978, many Indian children were removed from home just because our parents or relatives were poor, illiterate, and powerless to stop it. Before that the BIA (Bureau of Indian Affairs) and the Child Welfare League of America (CWLA) thought Indian kids without parents would be better off living in white foster or adoptive homes. Due to this collusion between the BIA and CWLA, thousands of Indian children wound up missing from their tribes and blood kin. Our grandmother and our uncle saved my sisters and me from being lost like that.

I could have been one of those lost kids in Montana in the 1940s or in the housing project in Seattle during the 1950s when the prejudice against us as Indians was really bad. In addition to that external oppression, our family's poverty and alcoholism led to childhood feelings of fear and self-shame for me. That's why I believe what Sherman Alexie wrote in *Reservation Blues* (1995, Grove Press) was a sad truth in Indian Country: "You ain't really Indian unless there was some point in your life that you didn't want to be."

The sad truth in those days was that most Indians who were light-skinned enough to pass for white would have done it. I had one aunt who did this. She left the reservation and never wanted to have anything to do with our family again. As John Contway kept repeating in his book, *Red Shadows of the Blood Moon*, "Every Indian story is a sad story."

So as part of my personal healing story, here's my sad truth. Back in those days as a parent-less, half-breed Indian kid on welfare I would have definitely tried to pass as white—if my Indian skin hadn't been so dark and my hair hadn't been so black. Pictures of me as a boy are evidence that even as a half-breed I was too dark to even try to pass. And my Indian half has always been the dominant part of my story anyway.

Nowadays describing myself as a half-breed would probably make the contemporary "Indigenous authenticity police" flame me on Facebook. I don't care. I know who I am, what I've seen, what I've learned, and what I've been through. Smallpox, George Armstrong Custer, Andrew Jackson, and all the other celebrated Indian fighters couldn't wipe us out, but the back-stabbing, envy, and negativity we Indians often direct at each other is what really keeps us down and inhibits our collective healing. In contemporary times we call this "lateral oppression." As Jillene Joseph (A'aninin), founder of the Native Wellness Institute, often says in her community workshops, "Hurting people, hurt" and "Healing people, heal." Today in Indian Country we can make a choice to heal.

This lateral oppression among ourselves (the "Indian authenticity test") goes something like this: . . . you didn't grow up on the rez . . . you don't look like an Indian . . . you don't talk like an Indian . . . you don't speak your language . . . you don't pow wow dance . . . you don't drum . . . you don't wear braids . . . did college make you a whiteman? . . . you aren't enrolled—and on and on and on.

At least my sisters and I have escaped the current most hurtful manifestation of lateral oppression in Indian Country—"disenrollment." Disenrollment means that a tribe can terminate tribal enrollment for their own community members over some technicality related to a long deceased ancestor who did or did not sign a treaty back in the 19th century. This is an extremely hurtful action that is usually caused by worry over casino dollars among gaming tribes. I hope this internal lateral oppression among ourselves will stop so we can better heal from our generational soul wound in tribal communities.

Fortunately, there has been an incredible renaissance for healing in most of Indian Country to counteract white supremacy, institutional racism, and generational oppression by the government. In my opinion this began in the late 1950s and 60s with the "Fish-Ins" or "Fishing Wars" in Washington state and really took off with the occupation of Alcatraz in 1969 and the takeover of Wounded Knee in 1973. This activist movement toward empowerment has greatly helped our collective healing.

Standing Rock in 2016 was the most powerful recent example of our awakening. Younger Indigenous academic folks are now calling this movement "decolonization." There are actually a little too many syllables in that word decolonization, in my opinion, for our everyday use. So far I haven't heard decolonization used at any pow wows or tribal council meetings or ceremonies I've ever been too, but maybe just like "self-determination" or "tribal sovereignty," we might get used to using it.

Before the late 1960s it usually just wasn't cool to be an Indian. However, I have witnessed a great rise in Indian self-pride during the past 60 years. This has contributed to a contemporary growth in tribal community self-governance and increasing economic and political power. We have been healing as Indigenous people and cultural renewal has been happening. This healing movement is also evidenced by increasing resistance to harmful natural resource extraction on our homelands. Standing Rock was the most recent dramatic incident to illustrate our growing empowerment.

Thankfully, the younger generation of Indians is really beginning to change the old self-hatred and helplessness narrative. Here in the Portland area, I've especially seen this since the start of organizations like the Native American Rehabilitation Association/NW (NARA) in 1970, the Native American Youth and Family Center (NAYA) in 1974, the National Indian Child Welfare Association (NICWA) in 1983, the Native Wellness Institute (NWI) in 2000, Red Lodge Transition Services (2007), the Indigenous Twenty Something Project (I20SP) in 2017, and the recent Wellbriety Movement in Portland (a local program affiliated with White Bison, Inc. that was founded by Don Coyhis, Mohican, in 1988).

The most impactful for my own recovery from alcoholism and healing has been NARA. I always say that NARA wrecked my drinking. That began in 1970 while I was still trying to be "a social drinker" and the first NARA director, Steve Askenette (Menominee), conned me into joining his board.

NARA began helping lots of Indian men get sober (only a few women were involved initially) without any funding for the first two years and the news soon spread back through the "Moccasin Grapevine" to Washington, DC. In the spring of 1972 an Indian man named Bob Moore (Quapaw), Executive Director of the American Indian Commission at the National Institute on Alcohol Abuse and Alcoholism (NIAAA), was sent to visit the program. Bob was so impressed with NARA that his office later sent out another Indian guy, Bert Eder (Lakota) to check us out later that year.

Bert strolled into a meeting with the Oregon Office of Addiction and Mental Health (AMH) at a state office building in Portland with a big cigar in his mouth, wearing a short sleeve shirt, turquoise bolo tie, western cut pants, and cowboy boots. A tall and rugged-looking Indian guy from Fort Peck, Montana, Bert just took complete command of the room. He was the strongest, most impressive sober Indian man I had ever seen— and not the kind of guy you'd want to cross or take on in a bar fight.

During this meeting Bert ordered the state AMH office to "help those two Indian boys" (he pointed at Al Smith and me) apply for federal program funding. The AMH folks immediately assigned a woman from their office to help me co-write NARA's first federal grant request to NIAAA and it was approved shortly afterwards during the summer of 1972.

The NARA board then hired an all-Indian counseling staff. The first office was around 30th and S.E. Division Street in Portland, and the men's residential house moved from Northwest Portland to a house on 14th and S.E. Division. Tony Peo (Umatilla), was the first paid director, Joyce Culbertson Nelson (Fort Peck Sioux), the first receptionist, and the first paid counselors were Charlotte "Sugar" Pitt (Warm Springs), Devere "Papasan" Eastman (Lakota), Rufus Charger (Lakota), and Shirley and John Thunder Shield (Apache).

Most of the NARA counselors were pretty active in the American Indian Movement (AIM) and the first AIM headquarters was at Sugar's house in SE Portland. Several of the original NARA staff members later took part in the takeover of the Portland BIA office in the fall of 1972 and the occupation of Camp Adair in Corvallis, also in 1972, as well as the takeover of Wounded Knee in 1973. FBI agents frequently were parked across from Sugar's place, and she even took out coffee for them one time. We all had a pretty good laugh about that.

With the infusion of federal funding, NARA was also able to secure state funding. During the 1980s Dr. Sidney Stone Brown (Blackfeet) became the director, she added a women and children's component to the in-patient treatment program and NARA has continued to grow.

NARA in the early 1970s started sobering people up by integrating Indian culture as an integral part of their treatment program. This combination of sobriety and culture was a powerful attraction to me. After my five "social drinking" eras (college, ocean lifeguarding and surfing, the Marine Corps, rugby, Indian rodeo), I knew I had a good place to go. That good place was to finally quit drinking for good and to embrace my own Native cultural practices more honestly. My association with NARA beginning in the 1970s allowed me to see how the combination of AA, treatment, and Indian culture could help me maintain my sobriety and continue my personal healing.

When I finally quit the booze at home at Fort Belknap in 1982, I felt an immediate sense of relief and gratitude. Without the guilt that comes from drinking, I could hang out with two awesome Fort Belknap tribal traditional elders, Max White (Assiniboine) and Joe Ironman (Gros Ventre). Both Max and Joe invited me to participate in ceremonies at their homes and my newly acquired sobriety allowed that. When I quit drinking during the early 1980s there were only a few of us at Fort Belknap who started to combine AA with our tribal cultural practices, but this has steadily grown.

In 1983, my friend Harvey King and I were the only ones at a tribal council candidate forum in Hays to identify ourselves as non-drinkers. Probably due to that public declaration of sobriety, Harvey and I received the most votes of the 12 candidates for tribal council. Then, with the first Intertribal Sobriety Campout held on the Northern Cheyenne Reservation in 1983, recovery among tribes in Montana really began to take off.

Before I quit drinking, I remember thinking that life without the booze would be really boring, but the opposite has been true for me. I've had a lot of sober fun since 1982, and my sober friends around Indian Country have provided the positive support and healthy connections that I sought all my life. Still, like any recovering alcoholic, there are times when I miss the ease to face social situations that alcohol initially allowed me. With alcohol as medicine, I could achieve temporary relief from the "eternal imposter syndrome" that I'd always lived with—never feeling good enough. I still had to learn how to live without alcohol, and like most alcoholics, it hasn't always been easy.

There are many times while driving back home to the reservation from Portland or Seattle when I miss the romantic illusion of stopping in for a few drinks at a cowboy bar in some isolated or out of the way places in Montana. Last summer I had to laugh that these little places I used to always stop at while driving home are now closed: the bar in Bonner outside of Missoula, another on the Blackfoot River east of Potomac, one at Loma on the Marias River, The Plainsman Bar east of Havre, the bar at Lohman near Chinook, and The Spa at Zurich. Did I contribute that much to their business when I was drinking that they're all closed now?

A couple of years ago at one of the annual Spirit of Giving conferences in Portland put on by NARA, there was a keynote speech by Dr. Eduardo Duran, the author of *Healing the Soul Wound* (2006, Teachers College Press). Dr. Duran talked about the belief among many Indigenous people that alcohol is a spirit. In this context, it is a negative force that shouldn't be allowed in our sacred Native cultural ceremonies. It is also a powerful spirit that shouldn't be challenged . . . just leave it alone. As Dr. Duran spoke more about it, as well as his own personal spiritual experiences, it really made sense to me. The alcohol spirit was too powerful for me to quit drinking on my own. I needed help from others and "a higher power."

That's why I had to finally accept in 1982 that I couldn't control my drinking and alcohol was too strong for me to quit without help. So, my little AA home group at Fort Belknap and my sponsor, Ozzie, became my higher powers. With their strong fellowship, acceptance, non-judgmental attitude and positive outlook on life I could finally do it.

Since leaving work with my tribe at Fort Belknap in 1987, I have found great support and comfort in the Indian AA groups in Portland and Seattle and the Native social justice and wellness groups in the Portland area. The only non-Indian AA group where I've ever felt comfortable is in one in Beaverton, Oregon. After my wife BJ took the journey in 2014, I moved to Beaverton to be closer to my son Erik and daughter Joy and their families and became more involved with the sober community in Beaverton. With my kids close by, a large and friendly Indian community in the Portland area, and continuing part-time work with the nine Oregon tribes, I'll probably be sticking around here for the foreseeable future.

Fort Belknap at over 800 miles away is just too far to live away from my kids and grandkids . . . and then there are the winters. You have to experience Montana winters to know how tough it is to survive in so many below zero days and nights. I might not be that tough anymore.

With sisters Avis and Marsha (1995)
Marsha Spence Furfaro photo collection

With some young Native healers in Indian Country at
the Portland State University School of Social Work (2017)
Caroline Cruz photo collection

Chapter 15
Healing with Horses

I didn't grow up with horses all my life like a lot of reservation kids who had parents and permanent homes. My sisters and I were raised by grandparents and an uncle who couldn't afford a house with land and horses at Fort Belknap. Before we moved to Seattle on Relocation in 1949, when I was in the third grade, I was usually riding with some uncle on the back of his saddle out in Hays at the south end of the reservation. I rarely got to ride on my own. Later, while I worked for two summers during high school on racetracks with my stepfather (Dear John) and we didn't get along, at least during that time I learned a lot more about horses. Then getting involved in All-Indian rodeos during the 1970s increased my knowledge and interest about horses.

In the winter of 2009, I started volunteering at a mustang rescue ranch in Dallas, Oregon called *Mustangs and MOHR* (*Mustangs Offering Hope and Renewal*). I began as a volunteer, but after a couple of years this developed into contract work doing therapeutic horsemanship workshops with the Oregon tribes. Since then I've developed business partnerships with my two main co-workers, Amber Jones (Cow Creek) and Mona Smith Cochran (Warm Springs).

We have now presented lots of therapeutic horsemanship workshops with hundreds of Indian kids from all the nine

Oregon Tribes. This even included some Indigenous youth from New Zealand in 2019. We also involved Native veterans at two workshops during the Veterans Summit which is held annually at the Confederated Tribes of Grand Ronde in Oregon.

It's not something I've often shared, but this all began with some dreams I started having about horses in the fall of 2008. In these dreams I was riding a sweet sorrel horse over some hills back home at Fort Belknap. It's pretty coincidental that these dreams started right after the summer of 2008, when I'd completed my last sprint triathlon. I had decided to give up triathlons at that time due to asthma, but I knew I'd need to find some other type of less strenuous physical activity to keep me moving and sober.

I didn't have a horse at the time, in fact it had been over 20 years since my foster son Anthony and I had three horses given to us by my cousin Warren Matte (Gros Ventre) at Fort Belknap. It was also that summer of 2008 at a pow wow in Grand Ronde that an old friend, Steve Vincent (Wintu), invited me to ride one of his horses that he'd brought to the pow wow there. It felt real good to be back in the saddle again, and maybe that's what triggered my dreams a little later.

That fall of 2008 I also happened to read an article in the Salem *Statesmen Journal* about a ranch in Dallas, Oregon that worked with neglected or abandoned mustangs and other horses. This really looked interesting, but being an introvert and not wanting to intrude, I put off calling the owner of the ranch for a few weeks. Finally, I got up the courage to call Debbie Driesner, the owner of the DD Ranch and founder of Mustangs and MOHR. Debbie called back right away and we set up a visit at her place, which is about 15 miles west of Salem and about one mile north of Dallas.

A few days later, Debbie gave my wife BJ and I a tour of the ranch and we all had a good visit. I really got a kick out of BJ's reaction to all this. The day we went there BJ wasn't sure she wanted to go and only decided at the last minute to come along with me. After spending only about 30 minutes at the ranch, however, BJ and I decided to sponsor one of the mustangs. That was so BJ . . . a quick learner and so full of enthusiasm. The mustang we sponsored (paid a monthly donation for her care) was a beautiful mare named Easy whose temperament really matched her name. Easy was a good instruction horse and she later became a great therapy horse that the tribal kids loved to be around.

After volunteering for a while mucking stalls, feeding horses, and whatever else Debbie wanted me to do, she asked if I'd like to help her "gentle" a new mustang that just arrived from the wild horse herd in central Oregon. I then spent some time in the round pen helping that young mustang named Willow overcome her fear and get used to humans. It's an awesome feeling when a wild mustang finally lets you touch him or her and follows you around without a lead rope. I'll always be grateful to Willow for sharing this with me. Shortly after gentling her, Debbie brought in a skilled young female trainer to work with her and Willow soon became a nice instruction and therapy horse.

One of the things that helped me with Willow was my previous experience riding wild horses in All-Indian rodeos at the Warm Springs Reservation in Oregon. In rodeos at Warm Springs, we rode wild horses that had just been rounded up on the reservation there. These wild horses were a little rough when you got on their backs in the bucking chute, but if you got bucked off they wouldn't try to step on you or run you over like the rodeo bulls do.

A few years later, I saw further confirmation that mustangs or wild horses are not naturally aggressive toward humans—unless some human has intruded on their space or has abused them. My understanding about wild horses was increased again through some horsemanship certification training at Standing Rock, ND.

Jon Eagle Sr. (Hunkpapa Lakota) provides certification training on *Becoming One with the Spirit of the Horse* at Fort Yates on the Standing Rock Sioux Reservation. During a training I attended there in May 2016, he took several of us out to a pasture where a good sized herd of one and two-year-old wild stallions were enclosed. He wanted to show us that we didn't need to be afraid of wild horses (what Jon calls "untouched horses"), even stallions. If we didn't get too close or act aggressively, these wild stallions just let us walk around near them before they casually walked off.

We then witnessed an awesome show of Native horsemanship. Jon explained that he was going to show us how his tribal members used to catch and train horses in the old days. He then calmly walked into the herd and began following after a two-year-old stallion that he had picked out. The horse would walk or scamper off when he approached, but before long he was able to put a halter and lead rope on it. The horse still pulled away and ran off a couple times before Jon caught it again, and finally the horse followed him without fighting against the lead rope. Jon then led the horse into a round pen at one corner of the pasture where he gently worked with it by waving the lead rope so the horse would run off in circles. Eventually the horse stopped running and slowly approached Jon. In only about 45 minutes from the time when he first approached the herd and picked out the stallion, Jon had that horse following him everywhere he went and it didn't want to leave him.

Being exposed to this type of Native horsemanship training was a life changing experience for me and most of the participants in Jon's workshops in 2016. Consequently, I had to go back to Standing Rock again in 2018 for a second training experience.

Both times when I went back, NARA in Portland also sent along a young prevention staff member, Natosha Spaeth, who now works with their horse therapy program. I've come to believe this kind of cultural practice can be a powerful healing method for our horse nations.

Jon Eagle had demonstrated for us the process called "joining up" with a wild horse. This is a big part of what Monty Roberts had written about in his powerful book called *The Man Who Listens to Horses* (1997, Ballantine Books). The book immediately became a world-wide best seller. Roberts also began showing videos of his work in "gentling" horses versus "breaking" a horse to get to get to the point of "join up" (the process when an untrained horse willingly follows you without a lead rope). Monty Roberts has been invited to give demonstrations of this process in many other countries. The Queen of England has even asked him to train her horses.

Since Monty Roberts' book came out describing the gentling process when training a new horse, as opposed to the old method of breaking a horse, this has really caught on all over the place. The thing is, Indians always knew about the gentling process, or "natural horsemanship," before white cowboys taught us about the rougher ways of breaking a horse through fear and dominance. In the old days before fences, our Indian ancestors had to catch horses the way Jon Eagle did and develop a relationship with horses based on trust rather than fear.

That kind of natural horsemanship, within a Native cultural worldview, is Jon Eagle's specialty at Standing Rock. In September 2019 the Confederated Tribes of the Umatilla Indian Reservation (CTUIR) sent eight tribal members to one of Jon's three-day trainings at Standing Rock. These tribal members were so impressed with Jon's approach of relating to horses that they invited him out to present a two-day on-site training at Umatilla in December 2019. This training hosted by the tribe was well-attended and the participants loved it. The tribe now plans to incorporate several of Jon's methods into their youth suicide prevention program called *Horse Medicine*.

There is another Indian guy I met in 2017 who is an outstanding professional horse trainer in the Native natural horsemanship method. His name is Thomas Smittle (Blackfoot/Paiute/Cheyenne), and he had a prominent part in a recent movie called *The Mustang* (2019). Thomas lives on a ranch near Custer, South Dakota where he continues to offer horsemanship clinics and acts as an advocate for wild horse conservancy.

These experiences working naturally with horses, which began for me in 2009, have helped maintain my recovery road from alcoholism and my own personal healing. As Jon Eagle says, "Everything about horses is healing." An Indian National Finals World Champion, Clint Bruisedhead (Blood from Canada) said at one of our Oregon tribal youth workshops, "Horses are my therapy." A famous horse trainer, Frank Lyons, said one time in a clinic I attended that "Horses only want peace." British Prime Minister during WWII, Winston Churchill, is credited with saying, "There is something about the inside of a horse that is good for the inside of a man."

I've found all of these sayings to be true. In addition, the old Native ways of relating to and honoring horses offers a different cultural perspective on looking at these magnificent spirit relatives. In the powerful video *Dakota 38* (2010, *YouTube*) a young Indian man explains the Native way that horses represent the Seven Sacred Directions. He said that the horse's four legs represent the four cardinal directions, the tail is the fifth direction that points to our Earth Mother, the ears are the sixth direction as they point upward to the heavens, and when we humans join with the horse we are the seventh direction. The horse spirit completes us.

My co-workers and I use this teaching during our horse therapy workshops with tribal kids and veterans. Our written one-page curriculum used for grant funding is below:

Native American Therapeutic Horsemanship, LLC Curriculum

We begin with a circle, traditional opening prayer, introductions and expectations, and explain how horses represent The Seven Sacred Directions.

The 4 Core Elements

- Learn equine behavior, safety, and how to establish trust with horses to overcome fear

- Learn in-hand work cleaning stalls, feeding, grooming, cleaning hooves, and leading prior to riding

- Learn saddling, bridling, mounting, reining, and riding to help bond with horses in an appropriate and safe manner

- Learn respect, patience, responsibility, self-confidence, and commitment to others through interaction with horses

We provide lots of encouragement and hands-on learning, and end with a circle to share what we felt and what we learned.

So that's it—a simple one-page description of Native horse therapy and how my co-workers and I see it work. Basically, the horse does the teaching. We are just guides to help along the natural healing process that horses provide. Below are some quotes from counseling staff at Native social services programs who have brought their youth clients to our workshops:

This process gives youth an opportunity to process trauma in their lives in a non-threatening and natural manner . . . .[she] attributed aspects of herself and her relationships to the horse, which allowed an outlet for unresolved grief and trauma.

. . . what a wonderful experience going to the ranch was for our kids . . . working with the horses brought a respect and calm to our kids that I hadn't seen before. It was wonderful to see this trust grow each few minutes they spent working with the horses and the volunteers. The experience was so rewarding that months later they are still begging to be brought back and connect with the horses again.

Two types of formal non-Indian certification I know of used in Oregon are Equine Assisted Psychotherapy (EAP) and Professional Association of Therapeutic Horsemanship International (PATH). Before attending Jon Eagle's certification training I had attended a few EAP demonstrations in Oregon. While I found them interesting and helpful, I see a few major limitations in using EAP with tribes.

1) A formal EAP program is very strict about requiring both an EAP certified and licensed therapist and an EAP certified horse wrangler on site during work with participants—tribes rarely have both of these professionals available.

2) It is strictly a ground program so participants don't ride horses and riding instruction isn't given—I think Indian kids and adults want to ride, it's as simple as that.

3) Training costs and travel is pretty expensive to send tribal members to EAP certification—I doubt that many tribes could afford it.

4) EAP doesn't have an Indigenous cultural base—I don't think health initiatives in Indian Country can be completely effective without a traditional spiritual component.

I don't want to completely discount this approach, especially if we "Indianize" an EAP session when working with tribal participants. In Oregon there are two EAP certified tribal members—Amber Jones (Cow Creek) and Mona Smith Cochran (Warm Springs). I work with both of them when presenting therapeutic horsemanship workshops with tribal kids and veterans. At my home reservation in Fort Belknap there are now three EAP certified tribal members: Steve Fox, Tescha Ann Hawley, and Toby Werk.

The second formal certification method I'm familiar with is the Professional Association of Therapeutic Horsemanship International (PATH). In my opinion, this approach is way more holistic since it includes lots of basic horse care and feeding, ground work, and then riding instruction as well. There are two PATH certified facilities I am familiar with and both have been very effective in working with Indian clients, Sycamore Lane Therapeutic Riding Center in Oregon City and Forward Stride in Beaverton.

The two Indian treatment programs that sent clients to Sycamore Lane are Cedar Bough in Lake Oswego and the Native American Rehabilitation Association/NW (NARA) in Portland. Both Cedar Bough and Sycamore Lane have since ceased operations. After Sycamore Lane closed three years ago, NARA has sent their youth residential treatment clients to Forward Stride. NARA sends their youth clients once a week to Forward Stride and one time they sent 12 adult Indians who are involved in their veterans program. The veterans loved it and NARA plans to continue this if more funding becomes available. In recent years many veterans' programs around the country are seeing the value of utilizing equine therapy, especially in cases of PTSD.

In Oregon a couple of tribes are working with the state behavioral health office to figure out a coding system for tribes to obtain reimbursement for equine therapy. This seems to be getting close to reality, especially with the Umatilla Tribe.

Back home on the Fort Belknap Reservation the two horse therapy programs on the reservation both occasionally receive some grant funding. On the south end of the reservation Toby Werk (Gros Ventre) is certified in EAP and has a program at his place called the Blue Heaven Guest Ranch. At the north end of the reservation Tescha Ann Hawley (Gros Ventre) and Steve Fox (Gros Ventre) are both EAP certified. Tescha and Steve have recently started a non-profit called the Day Eagle Hope Project.

I'm not the most experienced and natural Native horseman in this business. As I said, I didn't grow up with horses since I didn't have parents who had their own land and could afford to keep horses. Doing this kind of work is just what my own destiny has led to. And I like doing it more than talk therapy. Yes, I've had years of pretty good experiences in one-to-one and group counseling, facilitating groups and teaching classes, but utilizing horses for therapy and teaching is what I've come to love.

I'd love to see more "horse nations" begin equine therapy programs on their reservations. If state governments and the Indian Health Service would reimburse the tribal programs for providing this Indigenous form of healing, I believe overall holistic health could be greatly improved in Indian Country.

When my wife BJ was nearing the end of her journey here I told her that I might not be able to afford to keep my horse, Koda. She replied right away that I had to keep him, that I would need him. BJ was right, Koda is one of my healers.

Koda, my healer (2016)
Kyla Merwin photo collection

Debbie Driesner and a NAYA youth (2011)
Caroline Cruz photo collection

Workshop at NAYA (2011)
Mona Smith Cochran photo collection

Horses and Instructors at Tribal Foster Youth Camp at Umatilla (2015)
Amber Jones photo collection

Equus International Film Festival with Monty Roberts
and Thomas Smittle (2017)
Photo courtesy of the Native American Humane Society

Chapter 16
Many Paths to Follow

Indians love stories. This one is mine—a parentless, half-breed Indian kid raised in poverty and growing up surrounded by alcoholism and institutional racism. A guy whose Indian half has always been the dominant part of the story. As a friend Big John Contway said in his book about the times of our childhood and our parents, "Every Indian story is a sad story. There was nothing expected other than living in chaos, poverty and alcoholic despair." (*Red Shadows of the Blood Moon*).

This story isn't over yet. I'm still above ground and have lived much longer at 79 years of age than a lot of other relatives and Indian guys I've known who were born on reservations. On one reservation that I'm very familiar with the life expectancy for a male tribal member was only 47 years just a few years ago. At another it was only 48 years on another two years ago. Alcoholism, domestic violence, unemployment, homelessness, car wrecks, homicides, and suicides contribute to the shortened lives of Indian men and women on many reservations.

It's estimated that 72% of Native Americans now live in urban or suburban environments (Joe Whittle, *The Guardian*, 4 Sept 2017). Did being a "city Indian" for most of my adult life save me from an earlier death on my reservation at Fort Belknap? Or did seeing the stark differences in socio-economic realities of white privilege vs. the poverty of us Indians in the city hasten my drinking and feelings of shame?

Dr. Tom Ball (Modoc) is a long time friend and former Chairman of the Klamath Tribes. He said twice during keynote speeches at conferences in Oregon that he doesn't agree with the idea about us Indians living in two worlds. He said vehemently during his speeches that "there's only one world!" Sorry, Tom, that's one point on which I have to respectfully disagree. For me, life on the reservation and life in the city have been two very different worlds. Growing up as a half-breed Indian and then working on my own reservation in contrast with what I have seen of white privilege in the city sure looks like two different worlds to me.

There is a world of white elitist wealth and power in the cities where dark skinned half-breed Indians like me and other people of color don't belong. White people in that world don't want to let people like us in, and they don't want to share their power. Every community organizing and activist event I've seen or been a part of have taught me that.

I don't belong in that world of white privilege and power, and I don't care. My Indian half is more comfortable and I have more fun within the Indian community and culture. I have told my AA home group that "You're my favorite white people," and I'm not totally joking. The white world is generally a pretty hostile place for us people with darker skins and different cultural values.

Some of my personal story has been difficult to write from a factual and emotional standpoint. Did I get the facts right, or did my memory fail me in a major way? Did I sufficiently protect other people's confidentiality, or did I share too much information? I hope not, and I certainly didn't want to bother or possibly embarrass some of the other characters in this story.

I've read and heard that writing one's own story is therapeutic and that has been true for me. I still have lots of regrets about mistakes I've made, and people or relationships I hurt during my immature and selfish drinking eras. I'm hoping that in 38 years of sobriety my deliberate personal apologies and living amends have been received as intended.

My grandmother used to call me "Traveling Wolf." She didn't understand my love of the open road, and it seemed to her that I was always moving around too much. To tell the truth, I didn't always understand why one path led me this way or that, but that has been my life in these times. I moved around so much during my early life, and still even during these later years, that a close Indigenous lady friend calls me "the Rez Rocket." She says I've always been moving around in my life, and I'm still on the road more than most of our other Indian friends who are around my age.

My first and main reason for writing this story was to leave a written record for my grandchildren and family in Arizona, Oregon, and Washington, and my relatives back home in Montana. My grandkids especially don't know much about their crazy old half-breed Indian grampa. There's the ego, of course, to leave a written story that I once walked this earth.

A second reason for this memoir was to honor and thank friends from high school, college, lifeguarding, the Marine Corps, rugby, Indian rodeo and those people during 38 years of sobriety who don't know the full story about their crazy half-breed Indian friend.

A third reason is that many of my friends and relatives at home in Montana don't know the back story of why I went home in 1980, and why I quit drinking there in 1982. It's pretty crazy that I would go back home at age 39 to an Indian reservation with a huge alcoholism problem when I knew in my heart that I needed to quit drinking.

Like most folks who have lived this long, and certainly most alcoholics, I hope I haven't left too much wreckage from the past and have tied up enough loose ends so my family and friends aren't left with a lot of debts or junk to clear up when I take the final journey. These are worries I have been having in recent years.

The other troubling thoughts or doubts I have almost daily are about my own spiritual beliefs and the afterlife. To an outside observer I probably wouldn't be called a traditional or spiritual person, and yet that's the way I turn to in my thoughts and prayers. I'm definitely not a Christian who attends a church building to pray and seek fellowship. Like lots of Indians, I still have too many resentments toward the Christian missionaries who beat their religion into my ancestors with the credo of "Kill the Indian, Save the man." Even today on my reservation and others there are still fundamentalist Christian churches that teach us we are sinners who must be saved to get to heaven. I hate how that dogma has belittled our Native beliefs and cultural practices and made us ashamed of our sinful dark skins.

I know for sure that when I check out for good I don't want any Christian church service or bible verses read. Sing a couple of hand drum songs, drink lots of coffee, eat a bunch of fried bread and soup, and scatter my ashes at Indian Beach in Oregon and in the Canyon at home in Fort Belknap.

As this path ends, I've also been hoping that I'm not too much of a burden to my family. I've also wondered more in recent years how this journey is going to end. I'm hoping there's a moment when facing the end of this physical life when I can leap into the next chapter as an adventure like other good ones I've had, especially with lifeguarding, rugby and Indian rodeo.

When I was in the lifeguard tower at Seaside and recognized that someone was in danger of drowning, it was a natural thing to shout down to the other guards "Let's Go!" The fear and adrenalin and excitement were all instantaneous. Later, when playing rugby, although it wasn't fear of death, there was still the fear of failure or injury when defending against the other team near our touch line (goal line), and it was natural to encourage my teammates with a shout of, "Come on, boys!" Then in rodeo when I was in the bucking chute on the back of a bull, it was natural to shout "Let's go, boys!" to the guys pulling open the chute gate.

When I take the final breath before the next journey, I sure hope to be able to shout out one more time, "Let's go, boys!"

Amber Jones photo collection (2015)

Acknowledgements

Thanks to Kyla Merwin at KMC Media for convincing me to tell this story, and getting after me to keep writing when I became discouraged about its value. Barb Graham and Carlyn Ramsey also supported and encouraged me. They helped get into print our friend John Wesley Contway's book *Red Shadows of the Blood Moon* (2016, Trafford Publishing). These two awesome ladies know Montana and the realities that faced Indians like Big John and me. Nico Wind Cordova helped a lot with her support and uploading the pictures. My son and daughter, Erik and Joy, and my sisters, Marsha and Avis, are my rocks.

Many friends, relatives, teachers, teammates, and co-workers who shared a path I was on at the time and were accepting and supportive of me are noted in this account and I want to sincerely thank them all.

And a special thanks to several others not mentioned previously in this narrative: Laura Angulo, Donovan Archambault and family, Philip Archambault, Paul Bad Marriage, Doug Barrett, Travis Benoist, Becki Bishop, Med Buck, Margarett Campbell, Bobby Lee Cochran and family, Bobbie Conner and family, Terry Cross, Caroline Cruz and family, Sean Cruz, Derwin Decker, Michael DesRosier and family, Tim Doherty, Anthony Doney, Kay and Patrick Eagle Staff, Kathy Fitch, Tami Foster, Scott Fraser, David Fullerton, Estevan Garcia, Sister George, Ann Goddard, Matt Gone and family, Judy Gray, Edward Halver and family, Ashley Harding, Janice Hawley, Ruben and Jackie Horseman, Ron Hudson, Rosanna Jackson, Laura John, Julie Johnson, JoAnn Kauffman, Jarvis Kennedy, the King brothers (Ching, Harvey, Kim, Mitchell, Richard), Dana and Lisa Leno, Shane Lopez-Johnston, Duane Many Hides, Joe Martineau, Jackie Mercer, Theda Newbreast, Jose Obra, Fariborz Pakseresht,

Jill and Delores Plumage, Kristen Potts, Loye Ryan, Eric Shirt, Phillip Shortman, Angie Simons, Michelle Singer, Paul Skyhawk, Woodrow Star, the Stiffarm family, Lydell Suppah, Ray Tate and family, Julie Taylor, Ted Teather, Stephanie Thornley, Bob Tom, Jason Umtuch, Kathy Van Raden, Dale Walker, Patrick Weasel Head, Denice Wickert, Butch Wolfleg, Monica Yellow Owl, Eleanor Yellow Robe, and too many others whose names escape me.

It's been a good ride—thanks to you all.

9 781736 384

143

About the Author

Originally from Fort Belknap, Montana, John Spence now lives in Beaverton, Oregon near his kids, Erik and Joy, and their families. He shares a small house near the city library with his roommate Angie, two dogs and two chickens.

He credits his recovery from alcoholism and 38 years of sobriety to the healing and wellness movement in Indian Country. At age 79 John still rides his horse Koda whenever old rugby and rodeo injuries allow it.

Amber Jones photo collection (2015)